PLYMOUTH IN 50 BUILDINGS

DEREK TAIT

AMBERLEY

To Tilly, the best dog in the world. Much loved, never forgotten.

First published 2024

Amberley Publishing, The Hill, Stroud
Gloucestershire GL5 4EP

www.amberley-books.com

British Library Cataloguing in Publication Data.
A catalogue record for this book is available from the British Library.

ISBN 978 1 3981 1839 3 (print)
ISBN 978 1 3981 1840 9 (ebook)

Typesetting by SJmagic DESIGN SERVICES, India.
Printed in Great Britain.

Contents

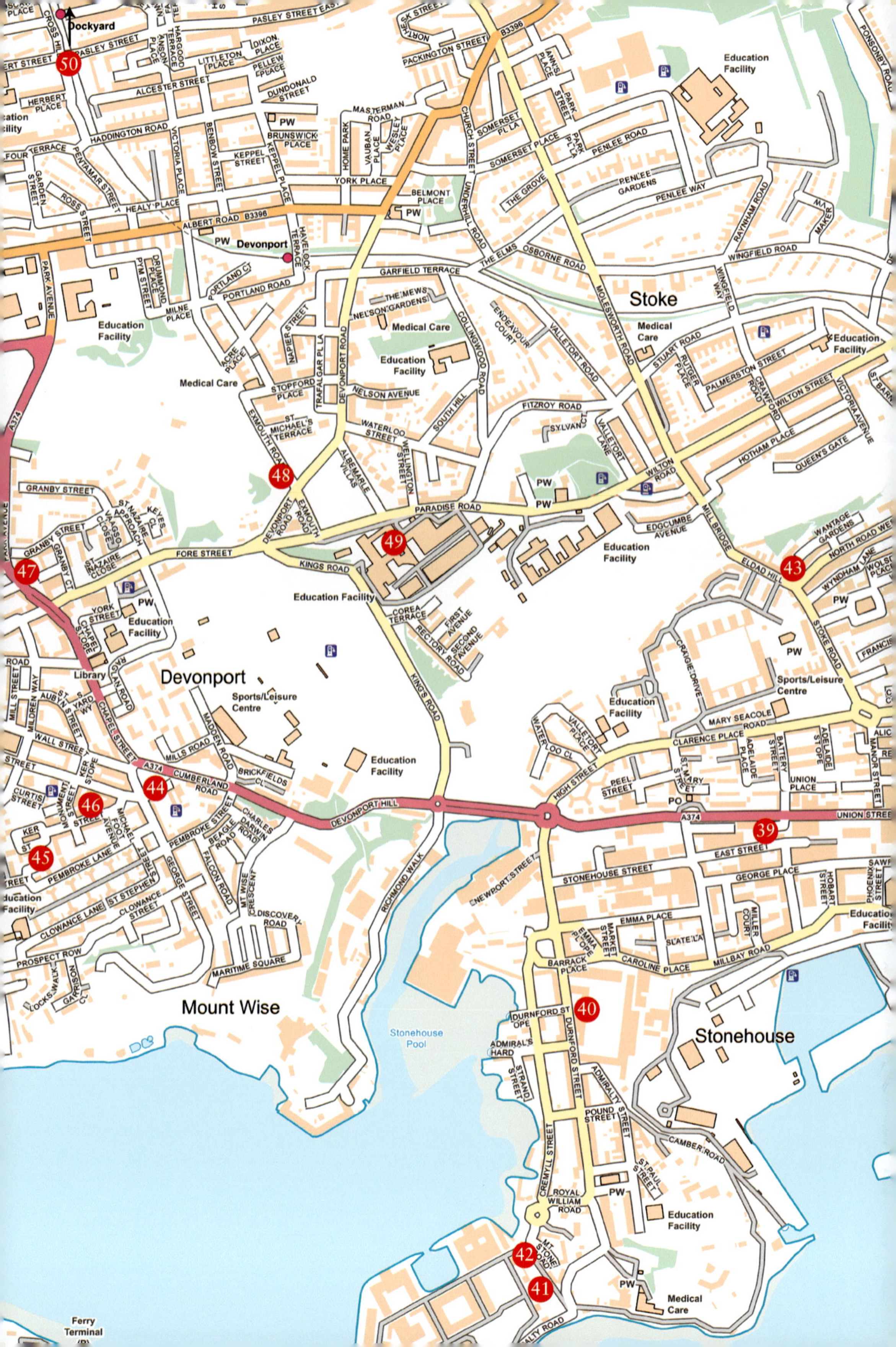
Dockyard
PASLEY STREET
PASLEY STREET EAST
CROSS HILL
HERBERT PLACE
ALCESTER STREET
HARGOOD TERRACE
ANSON PLACE
LITTLETON PLACE
DIXON PLACE
PELLEW PLACE
DUNDONALD STREET
NORTHESK STREET
PACKINGTON STREET
B3396
MASTERMAN ROAD
HADDINGTON ROAD
VICTORIA PLACE
BENBOW STREET
KEPPEL STREET
KEPPEL PLACE
BRUNSWICK PLACE
PW
HOME PARK
VAUBAN PLACE
WESLEY PLACE
CHURCH STREET
SOMERSET PL LA
SOMERSET PLACE
ANN'S PLACE
PARK STREET
PARK PL LA
PENLEE ROAD
PENLEE GARDENS
PENLEE WAY
Education Facility
FOUR TERRACE
GARDEN STREET
PENTAMAR STREET
ROSS STREET
HEALY PLACE
YORK PLACE
BELMONT PLACE
UNDERHILL ROAD
THE GROVE
RAYNHAM ROAD
MAKER
ALBERT ROAD B3396
Devonport
HAVELOCK TERRACE
THE ELMS
OSBORNE ROAD
WINGFIELD ROAD
PARK AVENUE
PYM STREET
DRUMMOND PLACE
PORTLAND CT
PORTLAND ROAD
GARFIELD TERRACE
THE MEWS
NELSON GARDENS
Medical Care
MOLESWORTH ROAD
Stoke
WINGFIELD WAY
MILNE PLACE
NAPIER STREET
DEVONPORT ROAD
COLLINGWOOD ROAD
ENDEAVOUR COURT
VALLETORT ROAD
STUART ROAD
RUTGER PLACE
PALMERSTON STREET
CRAWFORD ROAD
ACRE PLACE
STOPFORD PLACE
TRAFALGAR PL LA
NELSON AVENUE
SOUTH HILL
FITZROY ROAD
WILTON STREET
VICTORIA AVENUE
ST BARN
A374
EXMOUTH ROAD
ST MICHAEL'S TERRACE
WATERLOO STREET
WELLINGTON STREET
ALBEMARLE VILLAS
SYLVAN CT
VALLETORT LANE
HOTHAM PLACE
QUEEN'S GATE
WILTON ROAD
GRANBY STREET
ST NAZAIRE APPROACH
KEYES CL
VIVAGSO CLOSE
PARADISE ROAD
EDGCUMBE AVENUE
MILL BRIDGE
WANTAGE GARDENS
NORTH ROAD WEST
GRANBY CT
FORE STREET
KINGS ROAD
ELDAD HILL
WYNDHAM LANE
WOLSDON PLACE
ST NAZAIRE CLOSE
Education Facility
YORK STREET
CHAPEL STORE
COREA TERRACE
FIRST AVENUE
SECOND AVENUE
RECTORY ROAD
CRAIGIE DRIVE
STOKE ROAD
FRANCIS
ROAD
Library
RAGLAN ROAD
Sports/Leisure Centre
MILL STREET
MILDREN WAY
ST AUBYN STREET
YARD WY
CHAPEL STREET
MADDEN ROAD
KINGS ROAD
WATERLOO CL
VALLETORT PLACE
MARY SEACOLE ROAD
WALL STREET
KER STREET
MILLS ROAD
BRICKFIELDS CL
CLARENCE PLACE
ADELAIDE PLACE
BATTERY STREET
ADELAIDE STREET
MANOR STREET
CURTIS STREET
MONUMENT STREET
CUMBERLAND ROAD
HIGH STREET
PEEL STREET
ST MARY STREET
UNION PLACE
PO
MICHAEL FOOT AVENUE
PEMBROKE STREET
CHARLES DARWIN ROAD
DEVONPORT HILL
UNION STREET
PEMBROKE LANE
BEAGLE ROAD
FALCON ROAD
EAST STREET
ST STEPHENS STREET
GEORGE STREET
NEWPORT STREET
STONEHOUSE STREET
GEORGE PLACE
HOBART STREET
PHOENIX STREET
CLOWANCE LANE
CLOWANCE STREET
MT WISE CRESCENT
DISCOVERY ROAD
RICHMOND WALK
EMMA PLACE
MARKET STREET
SLATE LA
MILLER COURT
PROSPECT ROW
MARITIME SQUARE
BARRACK PLACE
CAROLINE PLACE
MILLBAY ROAD
LOCKS WALK
GARRISON CL
Mount Wise
DURNFORD ST OPE
DURNFORD STREET
Stonehouse Pool
Stonehouse
ADMIRAL'S HARD
STRAND STREET
ADMIRALTY STREET
POUND STREET
CAMBER ROAD
CREMYLL STREET
ST PAUL STREET
ROYAL WILLIAM ROAD
MT STONE ROAD
Ferry Terminal
39
40
41
42
43
44
45
46
47
48
49
50

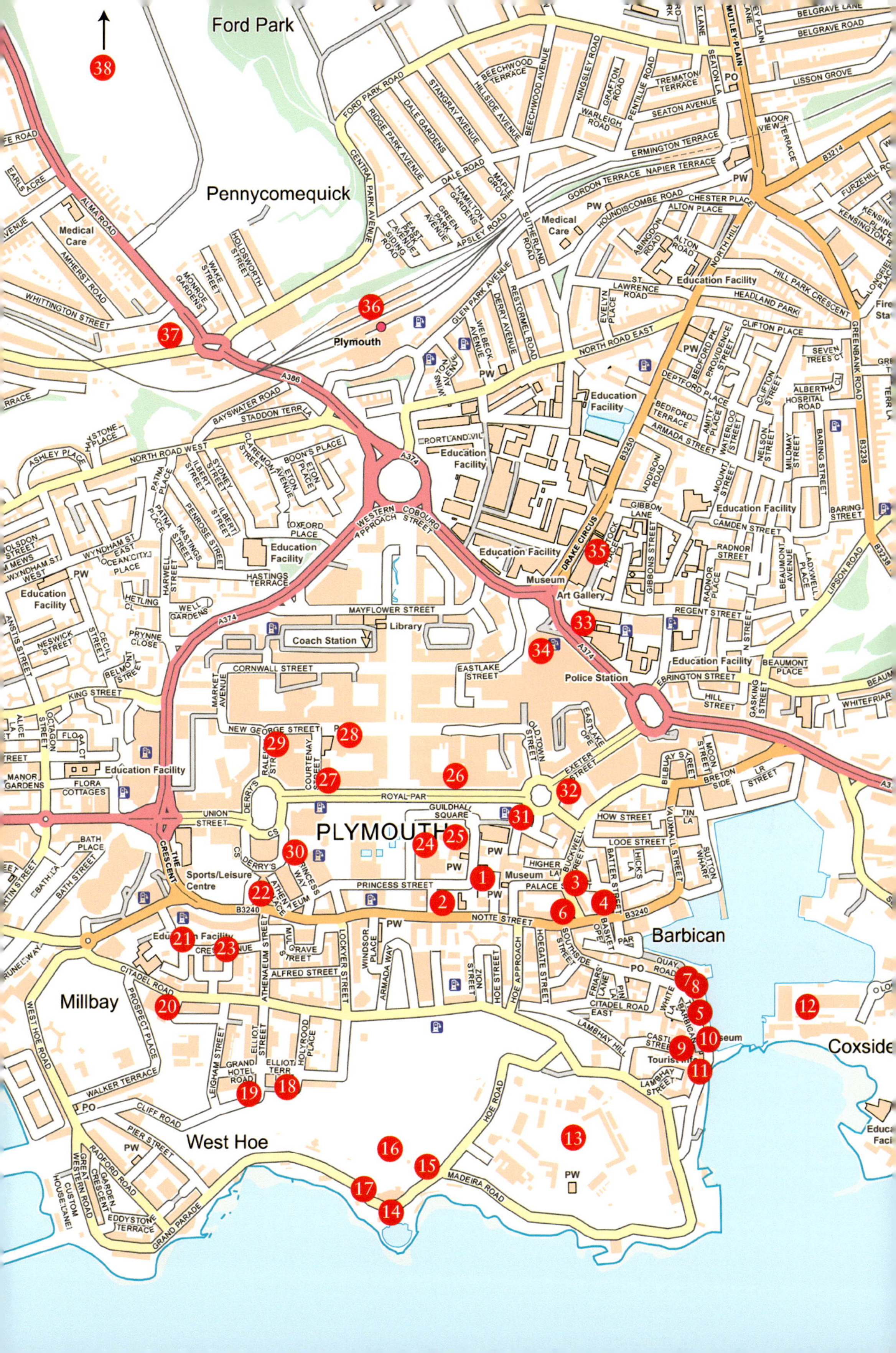

Ford Park
Pennycomequick
Plymouth
PLYMOUTH
Millbay
West Hoe
Barbican
Coxside
Medical Care
Education Facility
Coach Station
Library
Museum
Art Gallery
Police Station
Sports/Leisure Centre
Tourist Info
DRAKE CIRCUS
MUTLEY PLAIN
ALMA ROAD
NORTH ROAD WEST
NORTH ROAD EAST
WESTERN APPROACH
COBOURG STREET
MAYFLOWER STREET
CORNWALL STREET
NEW GEORGE STREET
ROYAL PARADE
UNION STREET
PRINCESS STREET
NOTTE STREET
CITADEL ROAD
HOE ROAD
MADEIRA ROAD
GRAND PARADE
EXETER STREET
EBRINGTON STREET
GUILDHALL SQUARE
A386
A374
B3240
B3250
B3214
B3238
1
2
3
4
5
6
7
8
9
10
11
12
13
14
15
16
17
18
19
20
21
22
23
24
25
26
27
28
29
30
31
32
33
34
35
36
37
38

Key

1. Prysten House
2. The Merchants House
3. The Minerva Inn
4. The Customs House
5. The Island House
6. Plymouth Gin
7. The Dolphin Hotel
8. Jacka Bakery
9. The Elizabethan House
10. The Old South Western Railway Offices Building
11. The Admiral MacBride
12. The National Marine Aquarium
13. The Citadel
14. Tinside Lido
15. The Marine Biological Association Building
16. Smeaton's Tower
17. The Dome
18. No. 3 Elliot Terrace
19. The Grand Hotel
20. The Duke of Cornwall Hotel
21. Plymouth Pavilions
22. The ABC Cinema
23. Plymouth Athenaeum
24. The Civic Centre
25. Plymouth Guildhall
26. The Dingles Building
27. The Theatre Royal
28. The Western Morning News Building
29. Plymouth Market
30. The Bank
31. St Andrew's Church
32. The National Provincial Bank
33. Charles Church
34. The Drake Circus Shopping Centre
35. The Box
36. The Beckley Point Building
37. Plymouth Railway Station, North Road
38. Plymouth Argyle
39. The Palace Theatre
40. Royal Marine Barracks, Durnford Street
41. The Artillery Tower, Firestone Bay
42. Royal William Yard
43. St Peter and the Holy Apostles Church, Stonehouse
44. The Old Chapel, Devonport
45. Devonport Guildhall
46. The Egyptian House
47. The Forum, Devonport
48. The Swiss Cottage, Devonport
49. Devonport Technical School
50. St Budeaux Parish Church

Introduction

This book contains fifty buildings, all instantly recognisable to Plymothians, which will be well known to most. All the buildings featured within its pages are still standing and all can be easily visited and explored by the reader.

Plymouth lost many beautiful and historic buildings during the Blitz of the Second World War but many included in this book outlasted the indiscriminate bombing of the city. It's amazing how many structures survive from the pre-war days.

Some of the buildings that were around when the Pilgrim Fathers sailed from the city in 1620 are featured including the Minerva, Jacka's Bakery, the Prysten House, the Merchants House and the Island House. Many structures stood during the time of Sir Francis Drake, Sir Water Raleigh and Sir John Hawkins and they would have undoubtedly passed by them during their time spent on the Barbican.

John Foulston (1772–1841) was Plymouth's leading architect for twenty-five years and was responsible for the development of Union Street. He also designed a couple of wonderful buildings within this book, these being Devonport's Guildhall and the Egyptian House in Ker Street. Many of Foulston's grand structures have been lost over the years including the Royal Hotel, Theatre and Assembly Rooms, which were built between 1811 and 1818. The theatre was demolished just before the Second World War to make way for a small cinema, later to become the ABC. Foulston's lost treasures include the Plymouth Athenaeum, which was completed in 1819, bombed in 1941 and later demolished. Its replacement, the current Athenaeum, is featured in this book. Other lost Foulston buildings include the Proprietary Library, built in 1812 and destroyed by enemy bombing in 1941, the Royal Union Baths, built in 1828 and demolished in 1849 to make way for Millbay railway station, and St Catherine's Church, which was built in 1823 and demolished in 1958. Foulston was also responsible for the many stucco-faced terraces and suburban villas scattered throughout the city.

The book begins at the Prysten House and follows a route which travels through the Barbican and the Hoe, and then through the city centre and out towards Devonport before ending up at St Budeaux, covering many of the city's best-known structures.

It features surviving medieval, Tudor, Georgian, Victorian and Edwardian buildings, as well as more up to date buildings such as the Drake Circus Shopping Centre, the Box and the Beckley Point Building. All are fascinating and of historical importance in one way or another. Some are loved and some may be loathed but they all contribute to the rich fabric of the city.

A map is also included so that readers can easily locate the buildings featured.

The 50 Buildings

1. Prysten House

Prysten House in Finewell Street is located to the rear of St Andrew's Church. It was built in 1498 by Thomas Yogge, a wealthy merchant who also paid for the tower of the church. It is one of Plymouth's oldest houses.

In 1501, Yogge, who was involved in the French wine trade, gave a hogshead of claret which was presented to Catherine of Aragon when she arrived in Plymouth from Spain after a difficult voyage across the Channel. Catherine travelled to England to marry Arthur, Prince of Wales. At Plymouth, she travelled to St Andrew's to give thanks for her safe journey. Thomas Yogge died in 1509. Prysten House was built using Plymouth limestone and Dartmoor granite and was extended in 1635. It has a gallery facing into the courtyard and the left-hand room contains a well. The street name Finewell probably comes from this.

A plaque on the building reads: 'This 15th century building commonly known as The Abbey was originally designated or used as the Prysten House or Priests' House pertaining to St Andrew's Church.'

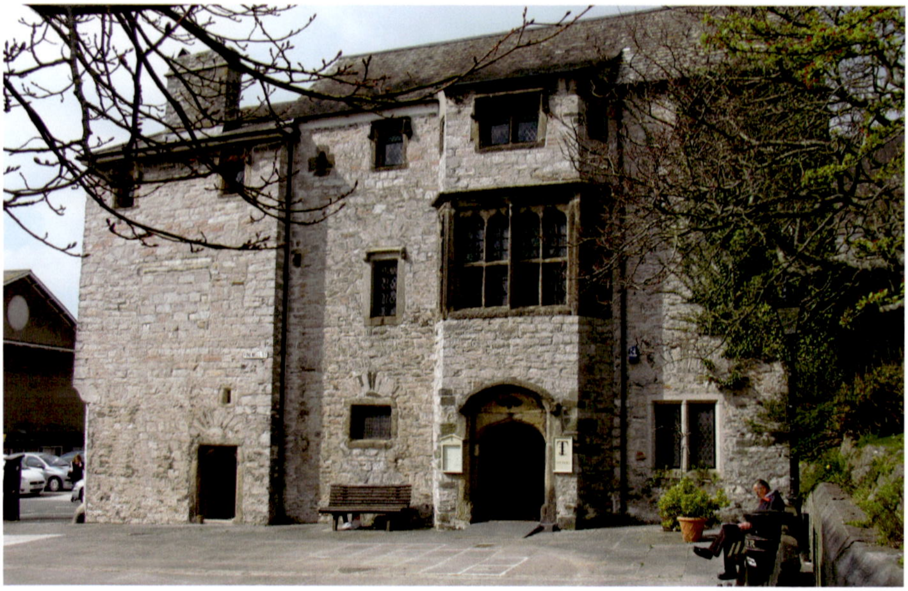

The Prysten House in Finewell Street.

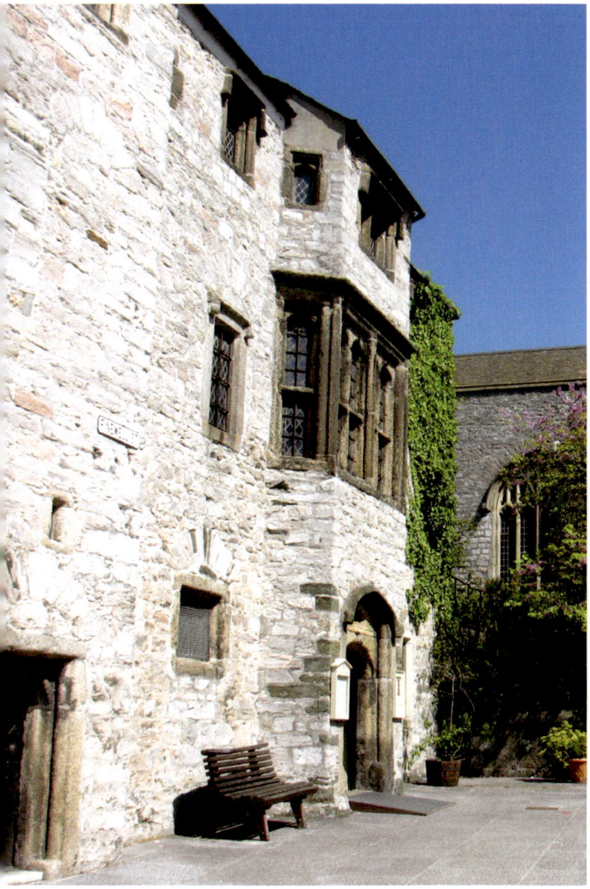

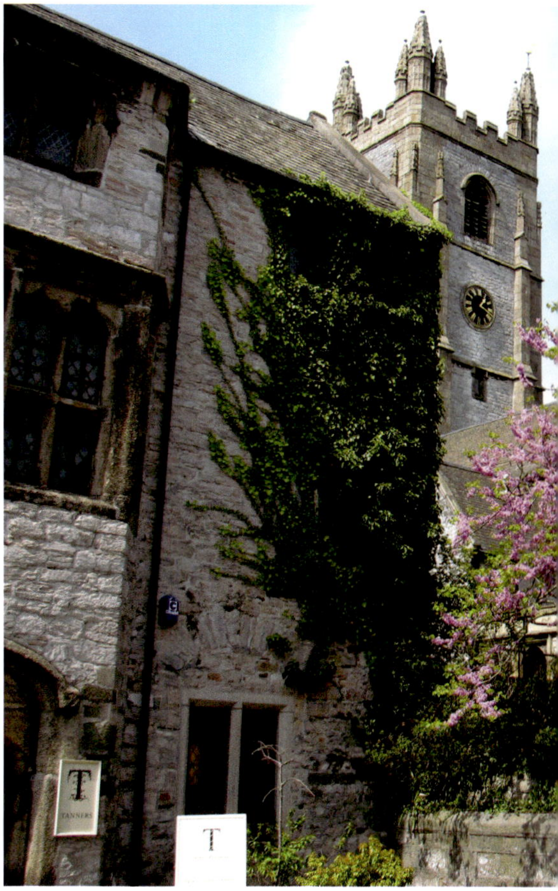

Above left: The Prysten House with St Andrew's Church in the background.

Above right: The clock tower of St Andrew's Church behind the Prysten House.

The house was greatly restored in the 1920s. The building was damaged during the Blitz in 1941. Today, Prysten House is owned by Plymouth City Council and is Grade I listed. In the past it has been used as a museum, a wine store, a warehouse and a bacon factory, as well as a restaurant. The Tanner brothers opened it as an eatery in 1999 and in 2014, it became the Greedy Goose restaurant. Prysten House is home to the Plymouth Tapestry, which was designed by Tom Mor. The project was conceived to help maintain the house by raising funds from visitor fees. Twenty tappissiers worked on the tapestry and gave their time for free. The work continued from 1976 until the end of the second project, which was the 267 feet by 4 feet New World Tapestry completed in March 2000. There is also a model which shows Plymouth in 1620. Another feature of the house is the Door of Unity, which commemorates the war of 1812.

2. The Merchants House

Originally built as a wealthy merchant's house in the 1600s, it replaced an earlier house which stood on the same spot in the 1500s. At least three mayors lived at the house including its first owner, William Parker. Parker was a respectable merchant but also a privateer who was good friends with Sir Francis Drake. In 1588, Parker served under Drake during the defeat of the Spanish Armada. He was in command of a victualling ship named the *Mary Rose* (not to be confused with the Henry VIII ship of the same name) during the conflict. Parker became Mayor of Plymouth in 1601 after capturing two Spanish treasure ships, which carried 10,000 gold ducats. He died in 1618 on a voyage to the East Indies but his family continued to live in the house until 1632. The next occupant was Abraham Rowe, also a successful merchant. The house was purchased by Justinian Peard in 1651. Peard twice served as Lord Mayor of Plymouth.

During the 1960s, the building was used as a taxi office before Plymouth City Council bought it in 1972 and restored it to its original glory and turned it into a museum. Part of the museum featured the fixtures and fittings of former family chemist, C. J. Park, who were originally based in Mutley from 1875 onwards. The pharmacy closed in December 1983. Other exhibits within the museum included a Victorian dolls house, nineteenth-century shop signs, manacles used to detain prisoners and a ducking stool.

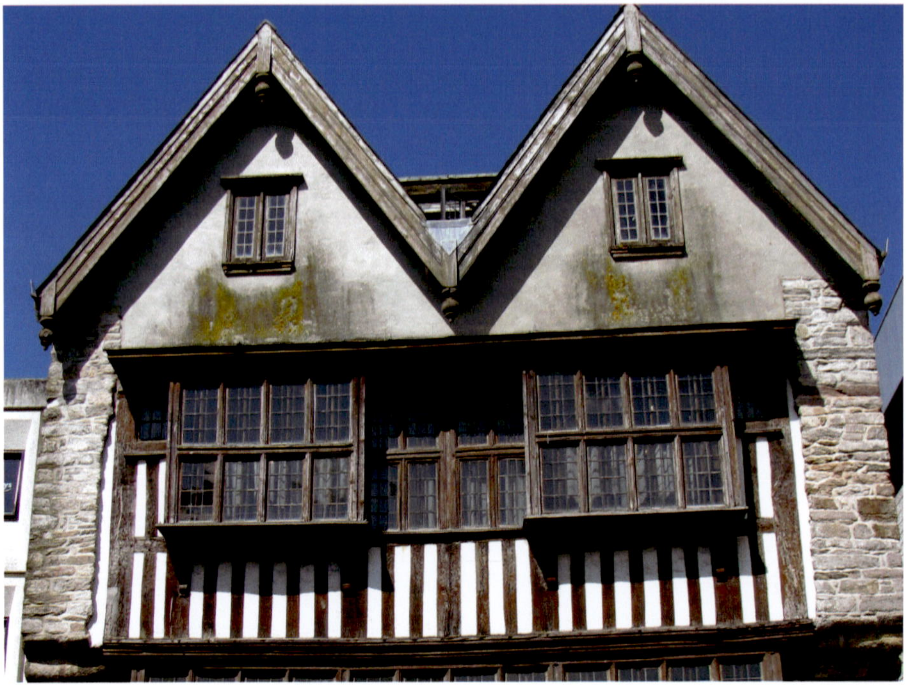

The top floors of the Tudor beamed Merchants House.

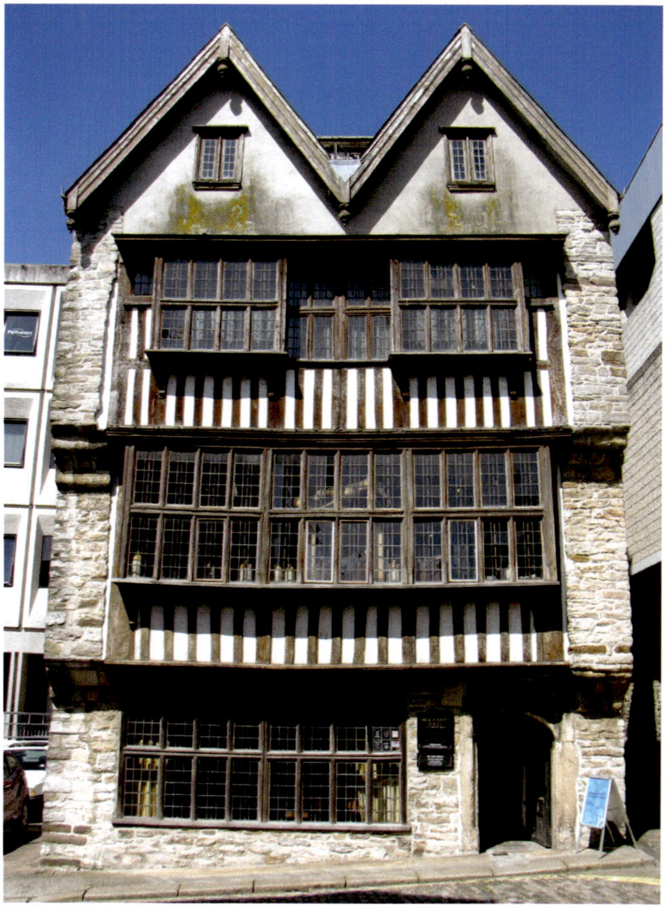

The Merchants House in St Andrew Street.

The house was a central feature of St Andrew Street which stretched from St Andrew's Church down to Notte Street. However, in the late 1970s, the Magistrates' Court was built right across the middle of the street, almost abutting the Merchants House, greatly overshadowing it and ruining the look of the street forever.

The seven rooms contained within the house were each dedicated to a particular period of Plymouth history. These include a Victorian schoolroom and a room which recreates the experience of Blitz in the Second World War in Plymouth. The museum is currently closed.

3. The Minerva Inn

The Minerva, at No. 31 Looe Street, is Plymouth's oldest public house and dates from 1540.

During the 1600s, the pub was home to press gangs who would drop the king's shilling into potential sailors' pints of ale, the men unwittingly accepting the payment and being led off to serve on various naval vessels. Secret tunnels and doorways are said to exist and a peephole exists where members of the press gang would spy on potential sailors. Some of the timber used in the pub is said to come from the Spanish Armada fleet, although the fleet didn't set sale until 1588 so would have had to have been added at a later date. The wooden spiral staircase is said to be made from the mast of a Spanish galleon and leads to a private residence.

The inn also boasts several ghosts spotted by many landlords and visitors over the years. Tales of a levitating spoon, cellar gas being turned off, the jukebox playing after it had been turned off and a small figure appearing beside the bar are some of the many spooky stories told.

The three-storey wood-framed building features a fine leaded window and a picturesque, large lantern. Minerva was the Roman virgin goddess of warriors, poetry, medicine, commerce, wisdom, crafts and the inventor of music. A portrait of her appears in the centre of the window in stained glass with the name Minerva above.

At one time, around the time of the Spanish Armada, Sir Francis Drake lived at Looe Street before moving to Buckland Abbey so he could well have frequented

Looking down Looe Street with the Minerva Inn on the right.

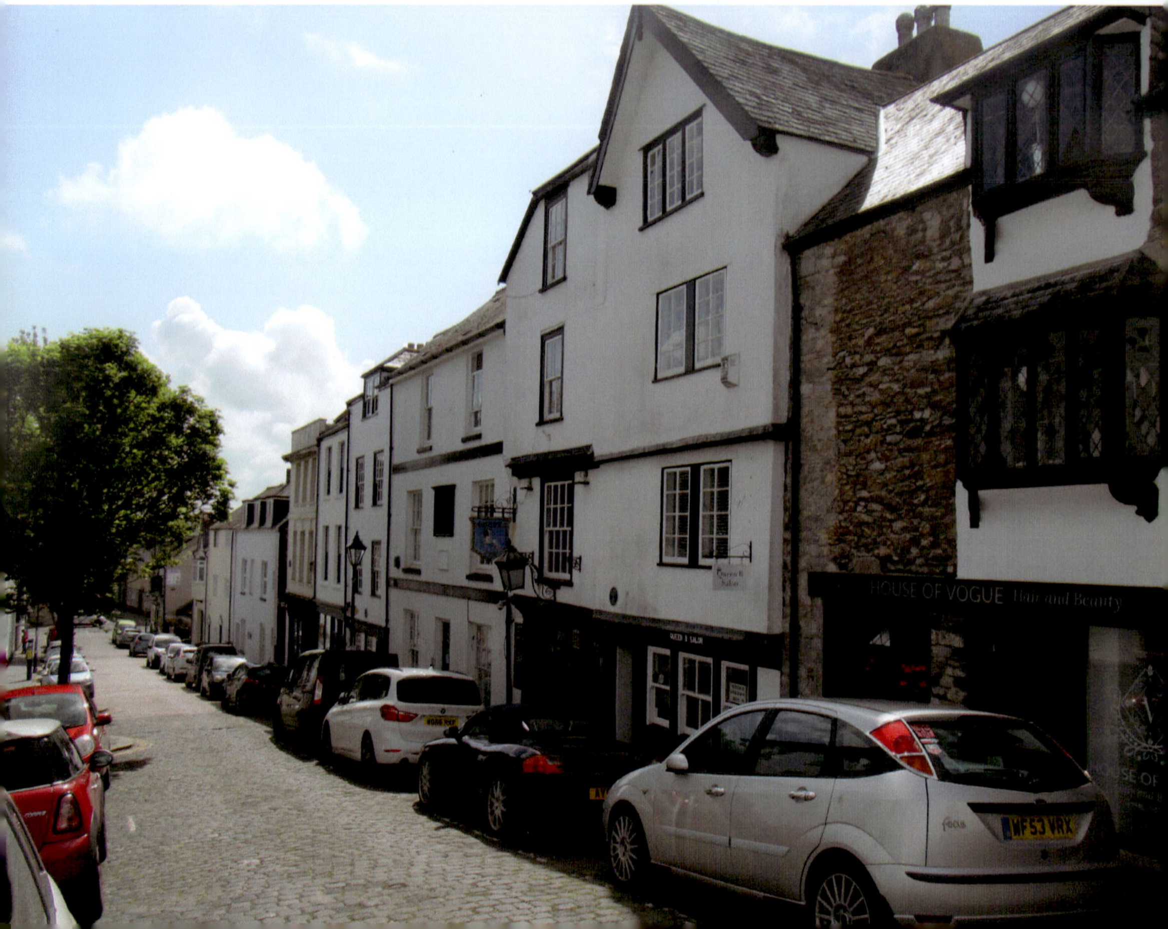

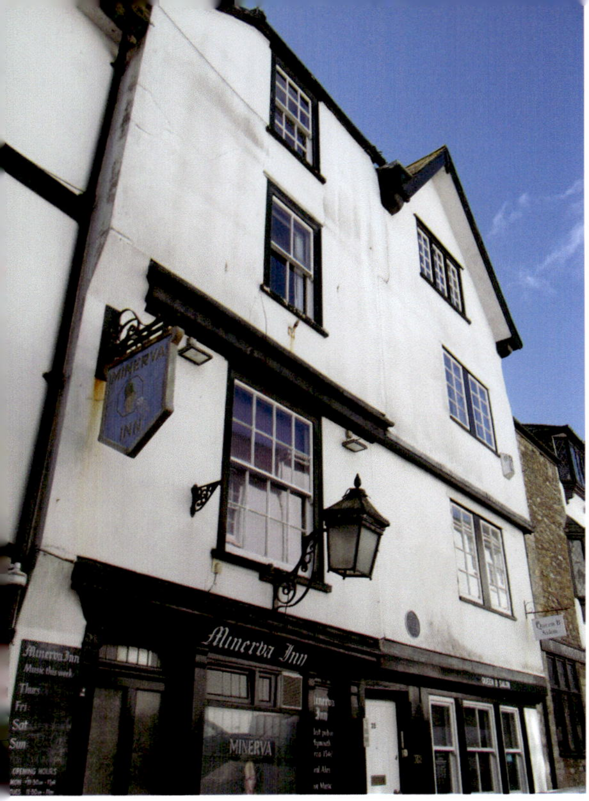

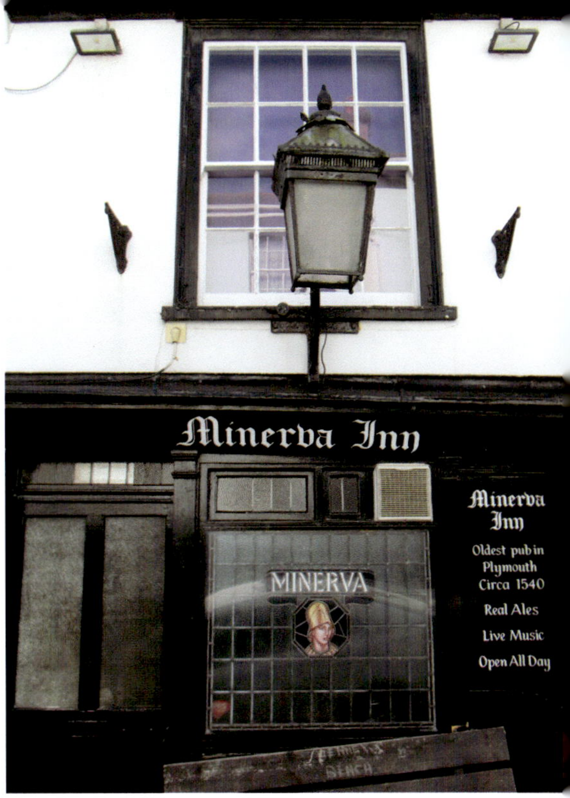

Above left: The frontage of the Minerva Inn.

Above right: The Minerva Inn showing the ornate light and stained-glass window.

the inn. The name of the street is said to have arisen from the fact that swine once ran loose there. It was also once known as Pike Street and housed the town's chief hotel, the Pope's Head. Dr Johnston stayed there in 1762 whilst on his travels.

Between 1861 and 1970, the owners of the Minerva were the Octagon Brewery, who traded in Martin Street. Their emblem still appears on the front stained-glass window.

4. The Customs House

The Customs House was built over several years using labour from Dartmoor Prison as well as French prisoners of war, who also worked on the Royal William Victualling Yard. It was designed by David Laing and completed in 1820. It was first occupied in 1823. The building is located at Guy's Quay on land reclaimed hundreds of years ago. Smuggling was once rife and the trade of contraband was very lucrative. The building was erected by a Mr Ball and has a frontage built of granite together with a colonnade of five arches. The stairway inside, also made of granite, led to the long room which adjoined the comptroller's and collector's offices. The building once had a stables and a Queen's Warehouse, where seized goods were stored and destroyed.

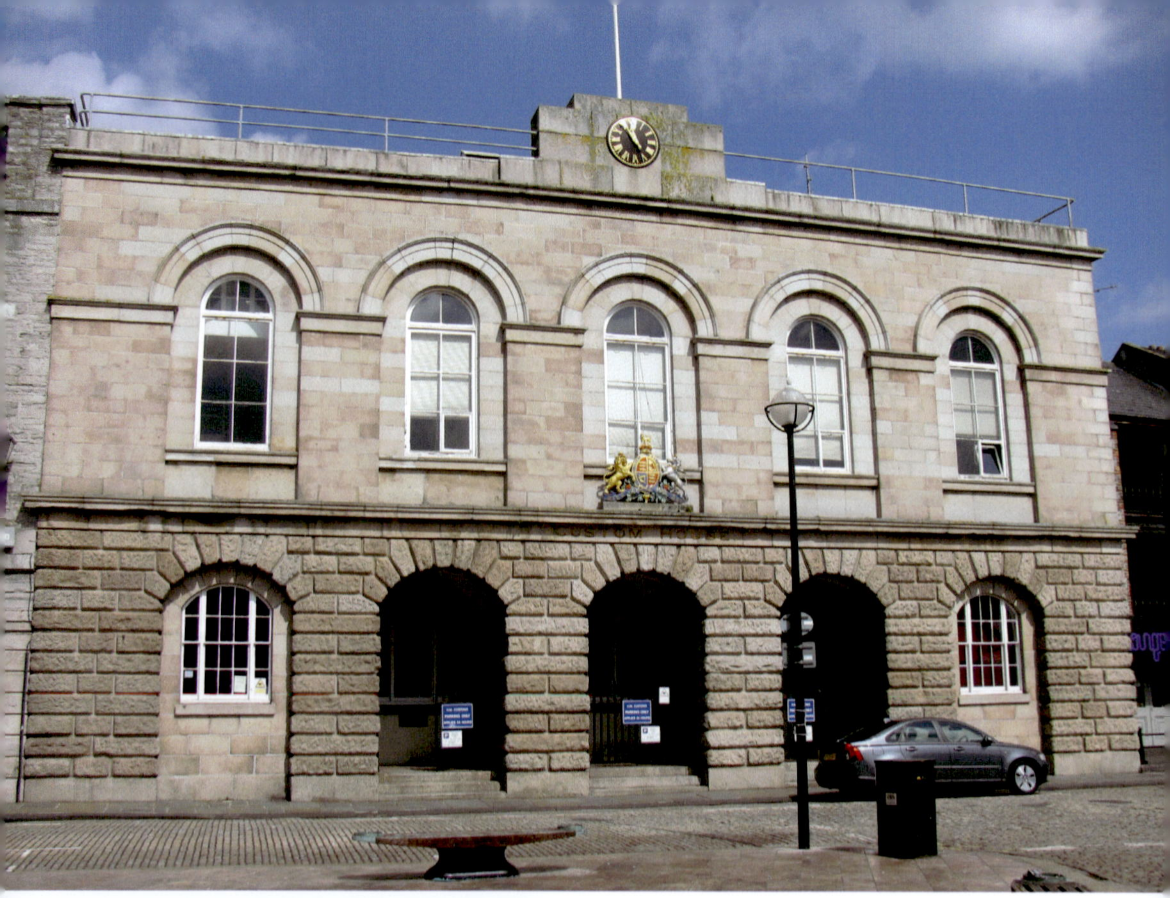

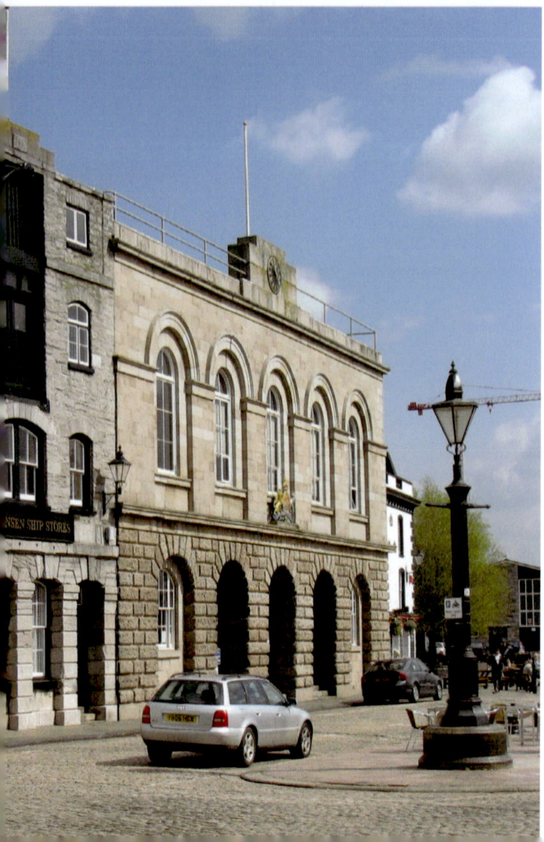

Above: The front of the old Customs House building.

Left: Looking towards the old Customs House towards the Three Crowns public house.

The ground floor housed the offices of the principal surveyor, tide surveyor, landing waites and searchers. The total cost to complete the building was £8,000. During the construction, one of the builders employed, Gribble and Hellyer, went bankrupt claiming they were poorly paid. The two-storey building features a black and gold clock and above the main entrance a coat of arms bearing the words 'Honi soit qui mal y pense', which translates to 'Spurned be the one who thinks ill of it'. The words are the motto of the British chivalric Order of the Garter, which is the highest of all British knighthoods, apart from in Scotland. The lion and unicorn crest also features the words 'Dieu et mon droit', which means 'God and my right'.

The Customs House served as an excise building for 190 years. In December 2010, customs officers left the Barbican after being located there for more than 500 years. Officers from HM Revenue and Customs and the UK Borders Agency moved to offices in Sutton Harbour and Ebrington Street.

Today, the customs house is occupied by a restaurant downstairs and a bar, restaurant and event venue upstairs. Internally, it retains many of its original features. The building is Grade II listed. The original customs house stood across the way and is now a bookshop.

5. The Island House

The Island House on the Barbican was built between 1572 and 1600 and was one of the houses that the Pilgrim Fathers stayed at before leaving on the *Mayflower* for America in 1620. The rear part of the house is thought to date back to the sixteenth century, while the front of the house was built in the seventeenth century when the quay was enlarged.

Robert Bayly and his wife Hannah leased the Island House from Sir William Molesworth in the early 1700s. Their son, John, moved to Plymouth in 1737 and joined Captain Brabant in his merchants and ship-owning business. When Brabant died in 1763 the business passed to John Bayly and in 1786, he purchased the freehold of Island House from Sir William Molesworth.

Island House stayed in the possession of the Bayly family until Mrs Emma Sophia Bayly died in 1924. She was the widow of Robert Bayly (1839–1901), who lived at Torr House, Pennycross, Plymouth. Elizabeth Mary Bayly (1870–1958) repurchased the house and in 1935 gave it to her nephew, John, to look after.

During enemy bombing on the night of 13 January 1941, the house suffered major damage. In 1948, John Bayley had the house restored by Messrs A. S. Parker and Allen.

On 11 April 1949, Island House was officially reopened by the Lord Mayor of Plymouth before it was leased to Messrs S. J. Lethbridge.

The building is Grade II listed. In 1976, a blue plaque was added by the shop entrance, which describes the Island House as 'one of the houses where a group

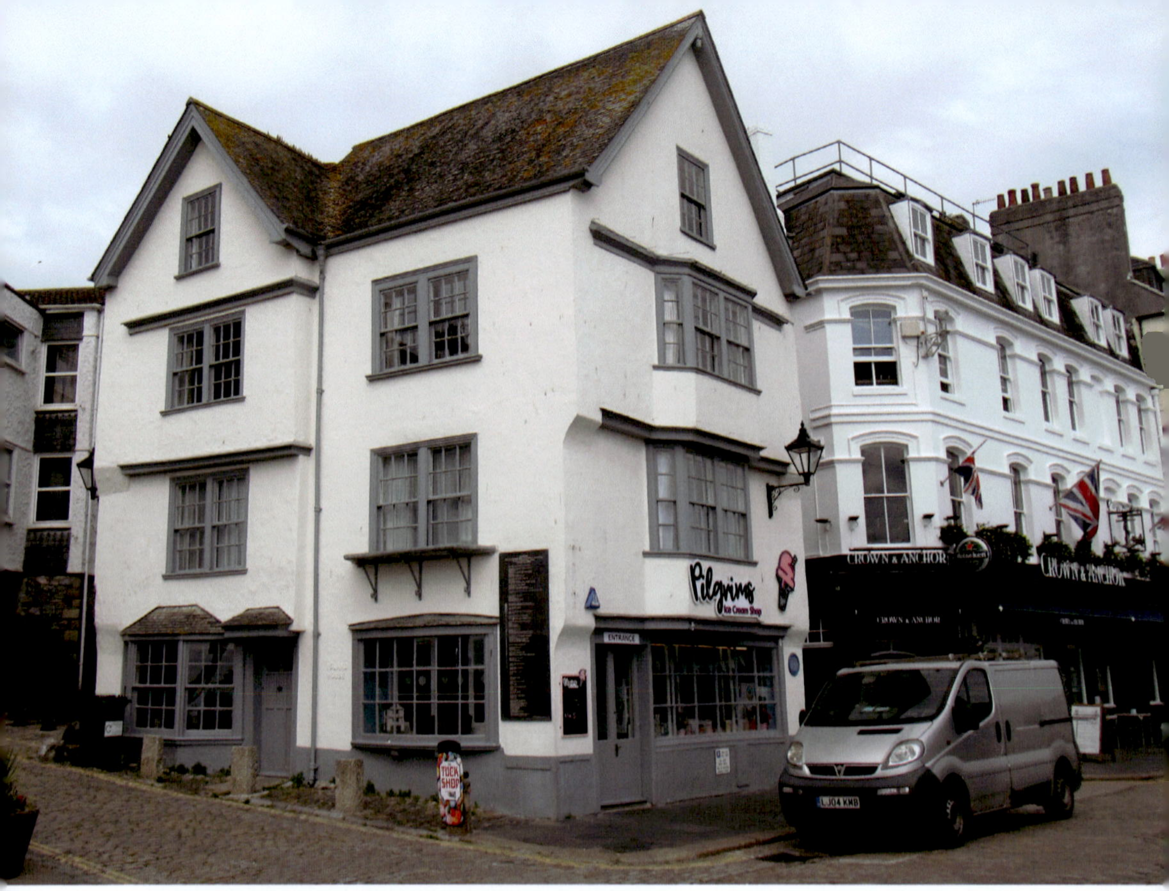

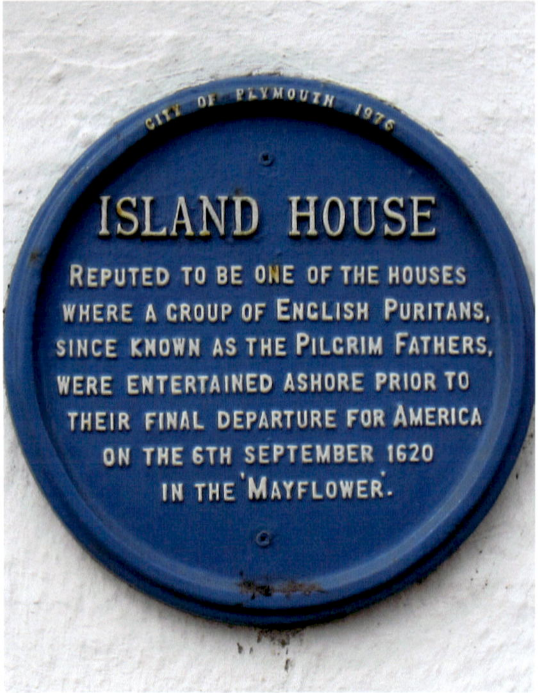

Above: The Island House, home of Pilgrims Ice Cream Shop.

Left: The blue plaque on the wall of the Island House.

of English puritans, since known as the Pilgrim Fathers, were entertained ashore prior to their final departure for America on the 6th September 1620 in the *Mayflower*'.

Also on the side of the building is a board with the names of the pilgrims who sailed from the Barbican on the *Mayflower* in 1620. This proves popular with American tourists searching for their ancestors.

Today, the building houses Pilgrims Ice Cream Shop. It was formerly a tourist information centre.

6. Plymouth Gin

The Plymouth Gin Distillery is the oldest working distillery in England and has been making Plymouth Gin since 1793. It is situated on the corner of Southside Street and Blackfriars Lane, although the tale of an order of Blackfriars inhabiting the building is apparently a myth.

The building on the Barbican dates from the early 1400s. The Refectory Room was once a medieval hall and features a fine hull-shaped timber roof which was built in 1431. It was formerly a monastery, occupied by the Greyfriars, until the Reformation and Dissolution of the Monasteries. It later became Plymouth's debtor's prison.

In 1620, the Pilgrim Fathers spent their last night there before setting sail on the *Mayflower* to start a new life in America. Today, the *Mayflower* appears on the label of every bottle of Plymouth Gin produced.

Records show that Blackfriars was used as a 'mault-house' as far back as 1697, although the distilling of Plymouth Gin only started in 1793 when Mr Coates joined the established distilling business of Fox & Williamson.

The original recipe for Plymouth Gin has stayed the same since 1793. During the Napoleonic Wars, Vice Admiral Horatio Lord Nelson ordered barrels of Plymouth Gin for his officers.

By 1850, the Royal Navy was being supplied with over 1,000 barrels of Plymouth Gin a year. It was often mixed with Angostura bitters or lime for 'medicinal' purposes.

In 1870, Plymouth Gin decided to perpetuate the myth of an order of Blackfriars once occupying the site and featured a picture of a friar on their label. In 1884, the company was awarded an injunction which prevented other establishments passing off their gin as Plymouth Gin. A case in 1887 showed that there were three other firms in Plymouth manufacturing Plymouth gin.

Due to the Royal Navy taking it onboard and around the world, it soon became the world's most popular gin with a thousand cases a week going to New York alone by the early 1900s.

Plymouth Gin is still made in a copper still that is over 155 years old.

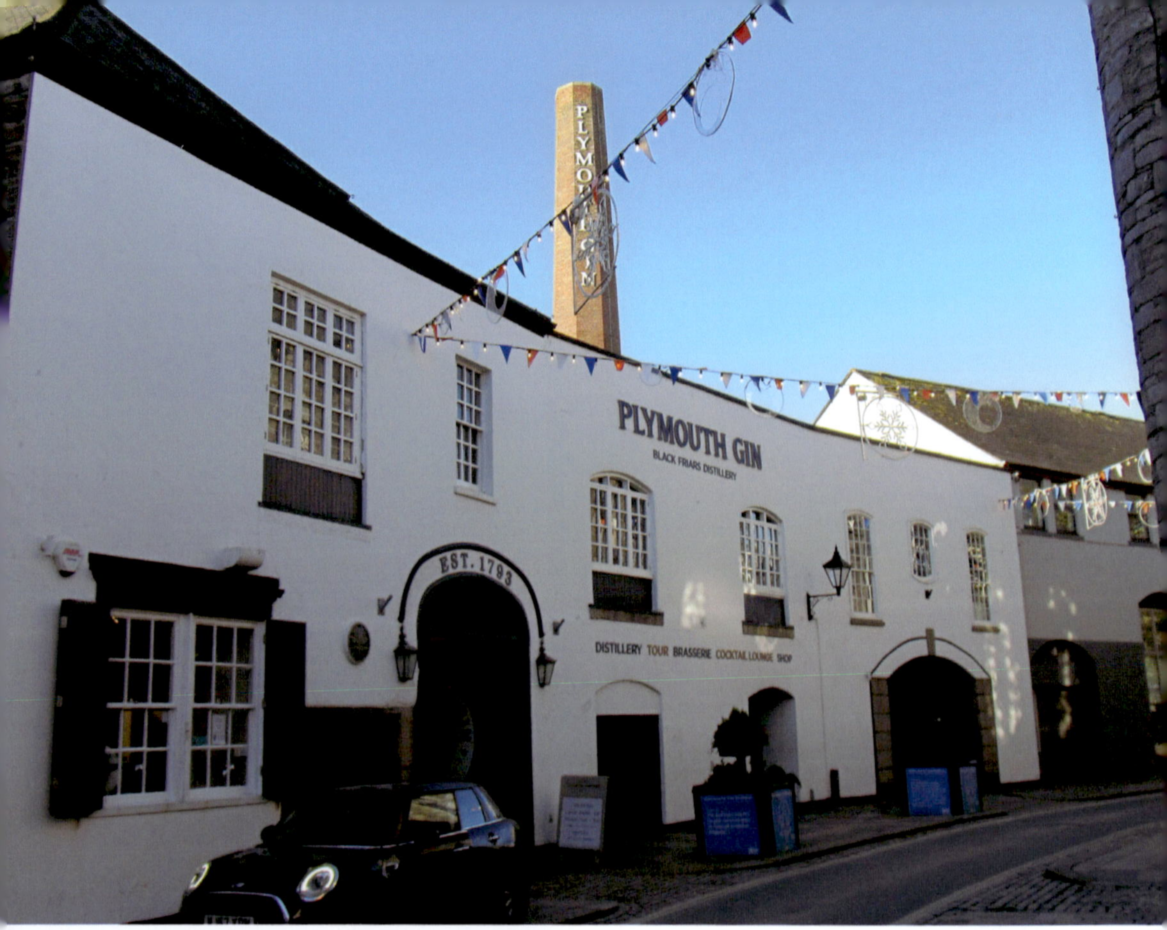

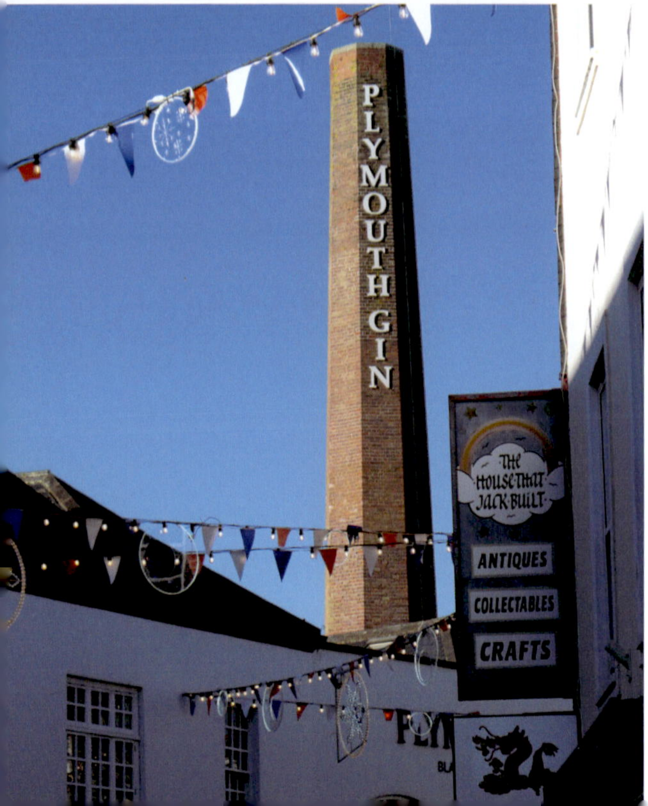

Above: The front of the Plymouth Gin building in Southside Street.

Left: The brick tower advertising Plymouth Gin.

7. The Dolphin Hotel

The Dolphin Hotel building on the Barbican dates from the early nineteenth century, although it may incorporate features from an earlier building. It's famously associated with the artist Beryl Cook, who featured the setting and its regulars in many of her paintings. Beryl Cook was born in Egham, Surrey, moved to Plymouth with her husband and bought a guest house on the Hoe. In the 1970s, one of her guests noticed her paintings and put her in touch with the Plymouth Ats Centre where she had her first exhibition in November 1975. The exhibition resulted in her being featured on the cover of the *Sunday Times*. That was followed by an exhibition at Portal Gallery in London in 1976 and her work continued to be exhibited there until she died in 2008. The interior of the Dolphin Hotel features Beryl Cook's paintings.

The Dolphin also has associations with several of the Tolpuddle Martyrs who stayed at the hotel in 1838 on their return from exile in Australia. At the time, Mr Morgan was the landlord. The martyrs who included James Loveless, James Brine, Thomas and John Standfield arrived in Plymouth on 17 March 1838 on board the ship *John Barry*. Huge crowds gathered on the quay at the Barbican before they were welcomed at the Dolphin Hotel. They later went to stay at the home of James Keast who was a prominent local trade unionist.

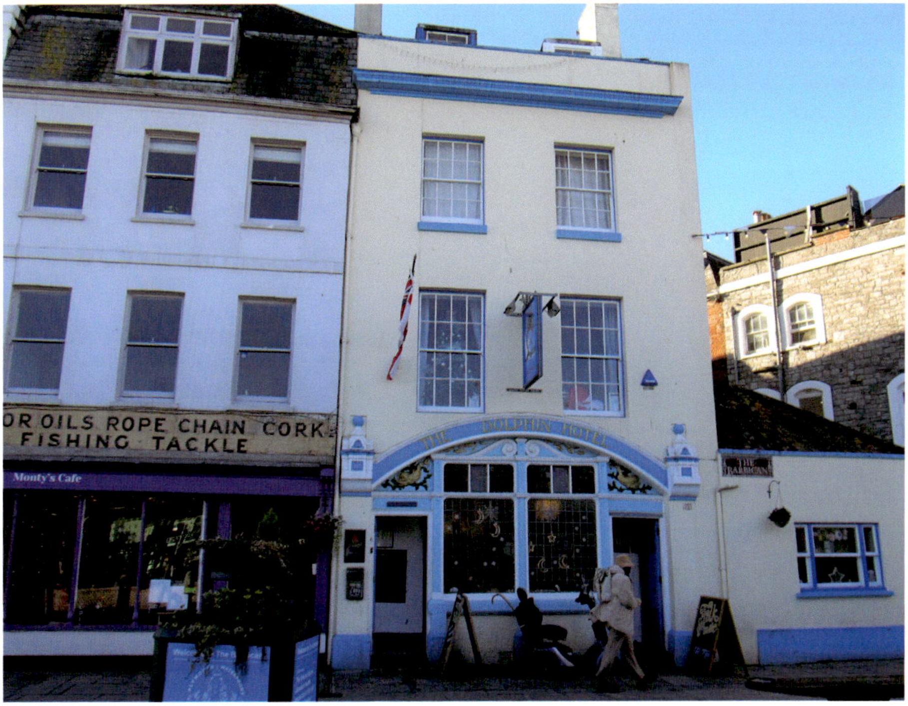

The Dolphin Hotel on the Barbican.

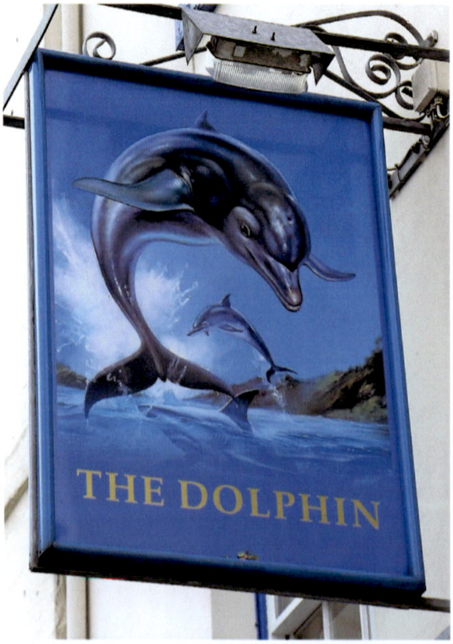

The pub sign above the entrance to the Dolphin Hotel.

The building is three floors high and features white stucco with plaster reliefs of dolphins. The slate mansard roof is surrounded by a tall parapet with a moulded cornice. The front lead lined windows feature the letters 'O B' in stained glass which stands for 'Octagon Brewery'. The inn is painted a distinctive blue and displays a pub sign featuring two dolphins.

An animated BBC comedy, Bosom Pals, was based on Beryl Cook's paintings and was set at the Dolphin. It featured the voices of Dawn French, Alison Steadman and Timothy Spall as the real-life landlord of the Dolphin, Billy Holmes.

The building is Grade II listed.

8. Jacka Bakery

Jacka Bakery at No. 38 Southside Street is the oldest bakery in the country dating back to the sixteenth century. The bakery was owned by the Fownes family in 1596 when wheat was 30 shillings a bushell. The bakery was there when Francis Drake, John Hawkins and Walter Raleigh lived nearby and they could well have visited the establishment.

It is said that the Pilgrim Fathers took biscuits baked at Jacka's on their journey when they set sail for America onboard the *Mayflower* in 1620.

In the early 1900s, the bakery was owned by F. F. Warren and the staff included his wife Kate. A well-known old photo of the shop taken in 1900 features Kate together with her children John and George. At the time, Hingston Brothers Blockmakers resided next door at No. 37.

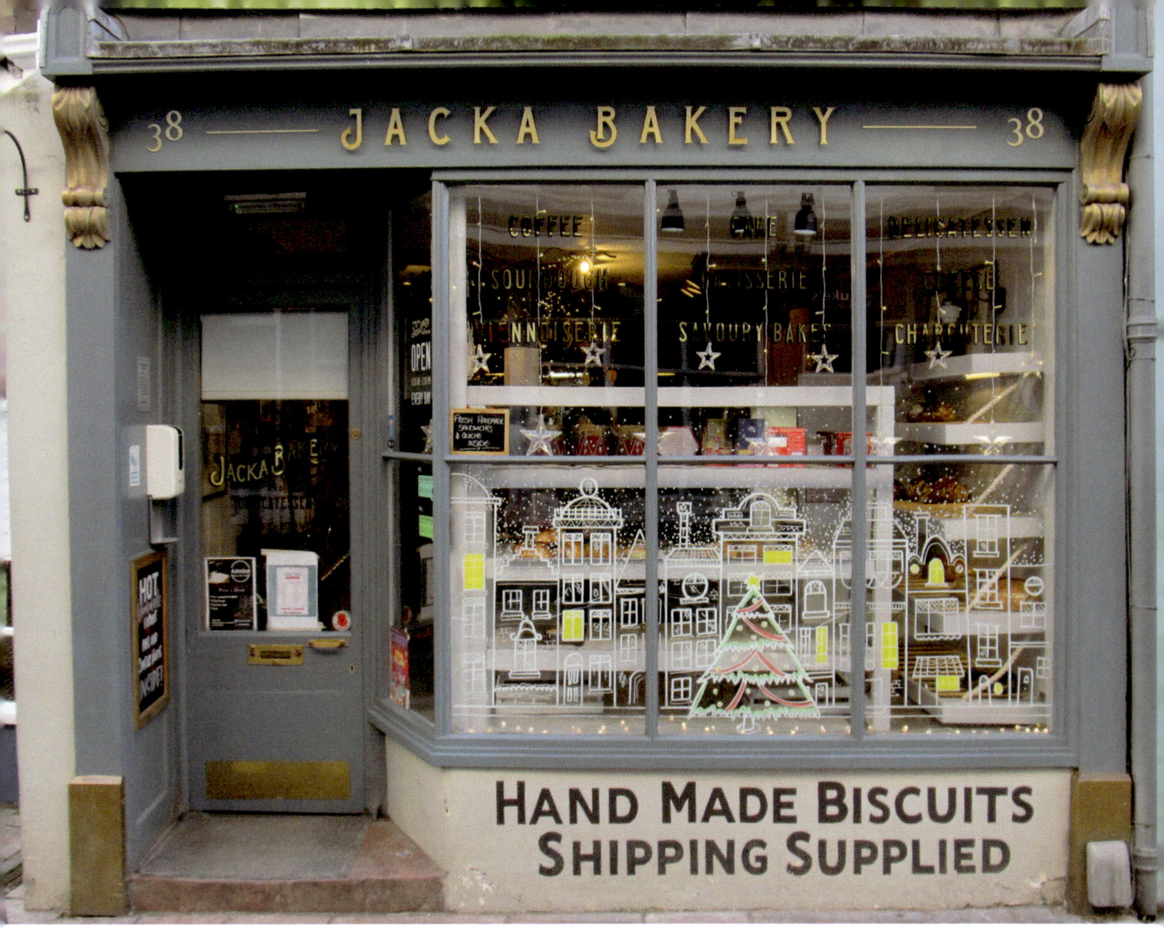

Above: The ornate window display at Jacka Bakery at No. 38 Southside Street.

Right: The frontage of Jacka Bakery.

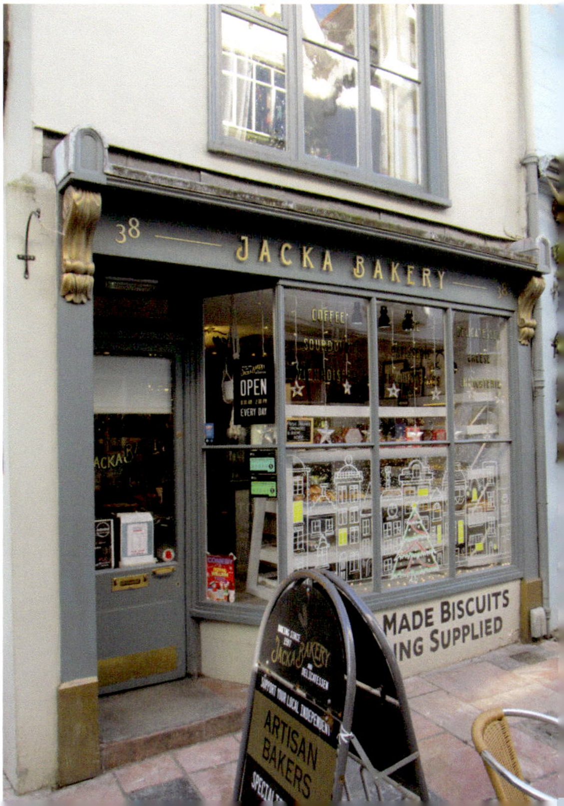

In the Second World War, many families who were affected by the heavy bombing of the city were allowed to use the ovens at Jacka's to cook their dinners.

The building is Grade II listed and features an Elizabethan balcony to the rear.

The shop has had several owners in recent years and was sold to the current owners in 2014.

9. The Elizabethan House

In 1584, the Mayor of Plymouth, John Sperkes, approved the building of New Street to house people who made their livelihood in and around the harbour. At the time, Plymouth was a thriving port.

William Hele was the first recorded occupant of what is now known as the Elizabethan House in 1631. He bought the dwelling from a merchant called Richard Brendan for £150.

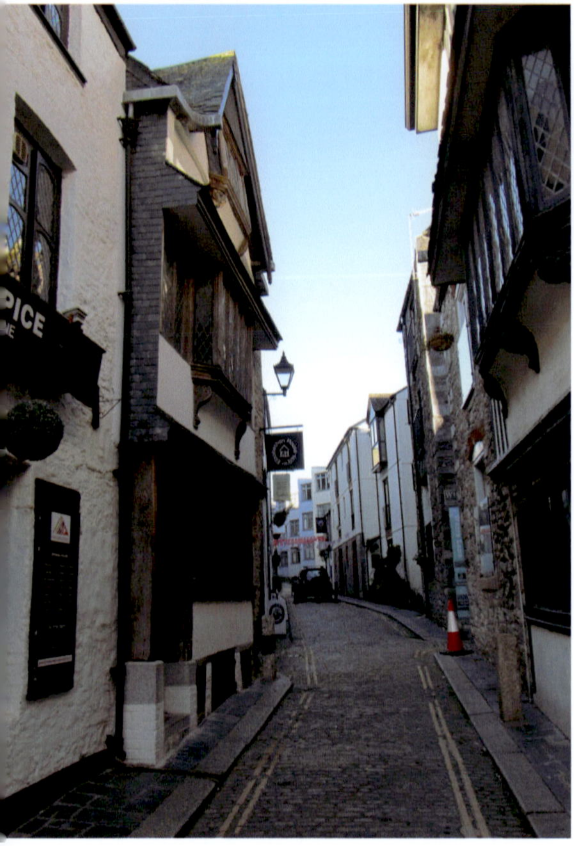

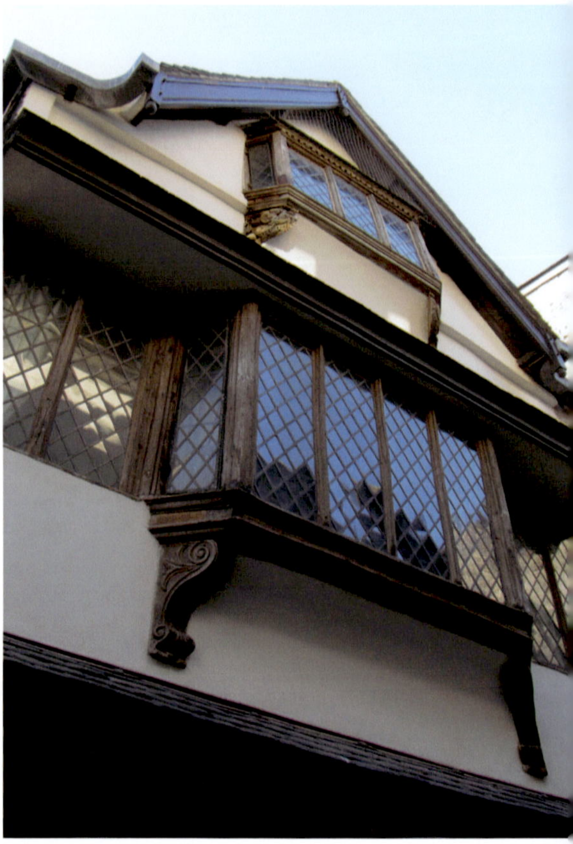

Above left: Looking up New Street with the Elizabethan House on the left.

Above right: The upper windows of the Elizabethan House.

In 1746, the London Company of Merchant Ventures were based there while developing and exploring the fishing grounds of Newfoundland.

At the beginning of the twentieth century, the Addison Housing Act identified nineteen different areas of Plymouth which it suggested should be cleared including the Elizabethan quarters. In 1929, the final occupant of the Elizabethan House handed over his deeds to the council for a demolition fee.

Local MPs, however, called for some buildings within the city to be reconditioned and the cause was promoted by the Old Plymouth Society, which resulted in No. 32 New Street being restored for the purpose of a Drake or Elizabethan Museum and handed over to the care and charge of the Museum Committee of the Plymouth Corporation.

The house is open to the public and also includes an interesting Elizabethan garden which contains small box hedges and herbs and flowers which would have been popular in Elizabethan times. The paths are cobbled and steps lead out towards Castle Street. There is a small pond with a fountain together with a sheltered area.

Walking beside the Elizabethan House at New Street, it's not hard to imagine Walter Raleigh, Francis Drake, John Hawkins or Captain Cook wandering down the narrow cobbled streets making their way to the busy harbour.

The house is reputed to be haunted. A child's cradle has been seen rocking upstairs and a small girl has reportedly been seen sitting in the corner of a room on the first floor, as well as being seen looking out towards the street from an upstairs window.

10. The London South Western Railway Offices Building

The building on the Barbican features its original signage, which reads 'London South Western Railway Receiving Office for Goods and Parcels to all Parts.'

The London South Western Railway Offices also stood adjacent to Derry's Clock in the early 1900s. The introduction of the railway changed the town, greatly allowing passengers to travel to Plymouth from other parts of the country, as well as taking passengers from the many arriving liners onwards to their destinations in London and elsewhere. The railway station at North Hill was opened by the LSWR in 1877, built jointly with the Great Western Railway. The following year, lines were laid between GWR's Lipson Junction towards a goods depot at Friary Green together with access to the Great Western Docks. In 1879, the Sutton Harbour Branch was opened, followed by the opening of the Cattewater Branch in 1880.

Plymouth continued to extend its railway and eventually had a sprawling network with many stations including the very busy one at Millbay.

In 1923, the London and South Western Railway Company merged with other companies and became the Southern Railway Company. The building was restored by the Plymouth Barbican Trust.

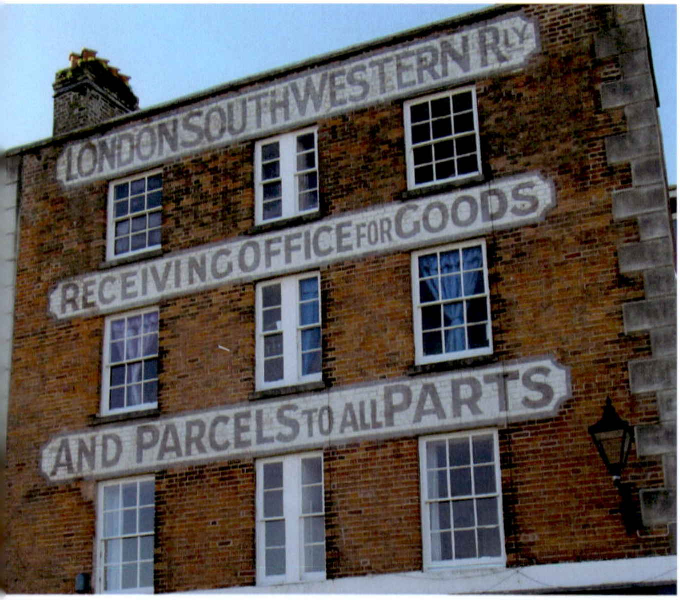

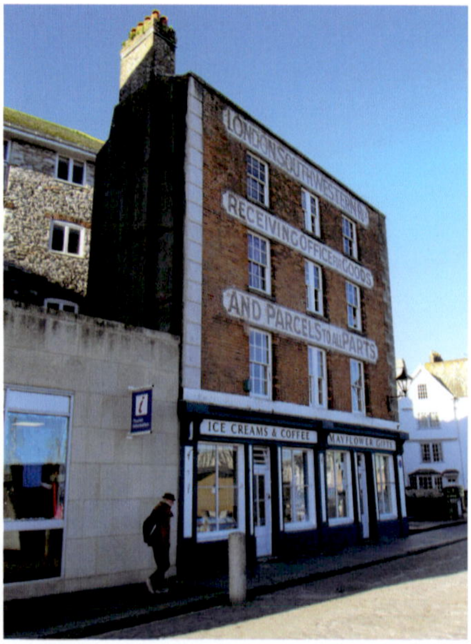

Above left: The signage on the London South Western Railway Offices building.

Above right: Looking towards the London South Western Railway Offices building with the Island House in the background.

11. The Admiral MacBride

The Admiral MacBride stands on the site of the original Mayflower Steps where the Pilgrim Fathers left for America in 1620. The harbour once stood further back and much of what you can see today is reclaimed land. Within the ladies' toilet of the public house is a marker showing the original departure point.

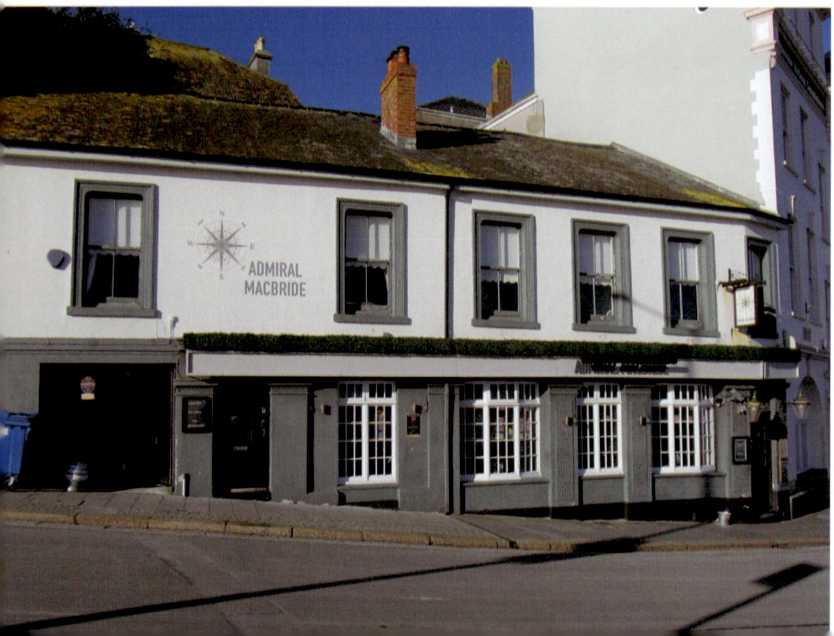

The Admiral MacBride public house.

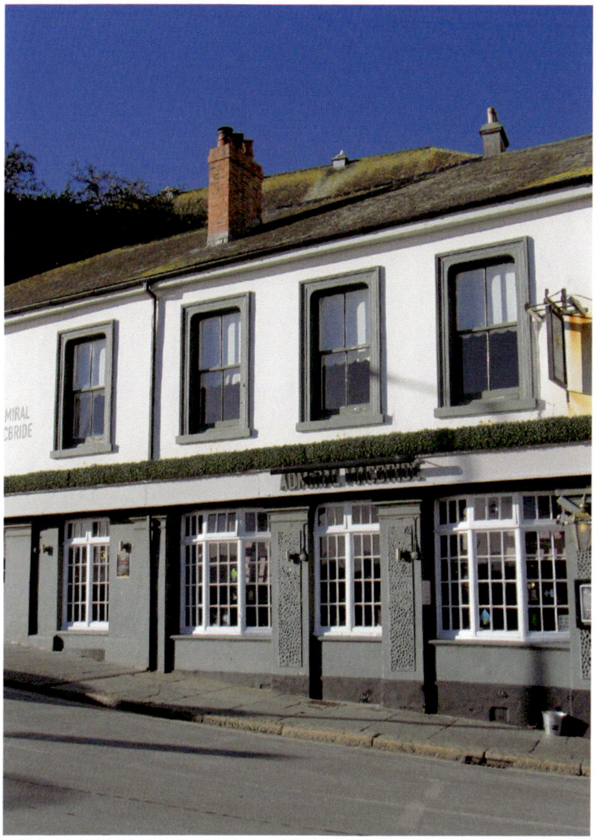

A view looking towards the Admiral MacBride. The harbour came back to this point when the Pilgrim Fathers sailed for America in 1620.

The inn was erected sometime in the late 1700s and was named after John MacBride (1735–1800), who was an officer in the Royal Navy as well as a politician. MacBride was born in Scotland and was the son of a Presbyterian minister. He served during the Seven Years' War, the American War of Independence and the French Revolutionary Wars. He rose to the rank of Admiral of the Blue. In 1784, he became MP for Plymouth and served until 1790. MacBride lived at Leigham House at the time. He was responsible for getting a bill through parliament which allowed the building of the pier that stands in front of the pub. Together with the eastern pier, it made Sutton Pool a safer place for ships to moor. In 1798, the licensee of the Admiral MacBride was recorded as Patrick Shea.

12. The National Marine Aquarium

The National Marine Aquarium was first commissioned in 1995 and opened its doors in May 1998. It was built on reclaimed land and is located in Sutton Harbour across the water from the sculpture the *Leviathan*, which is known more commonly locally as the Giant Prawn. It was designed by metalworker Brian Fell.

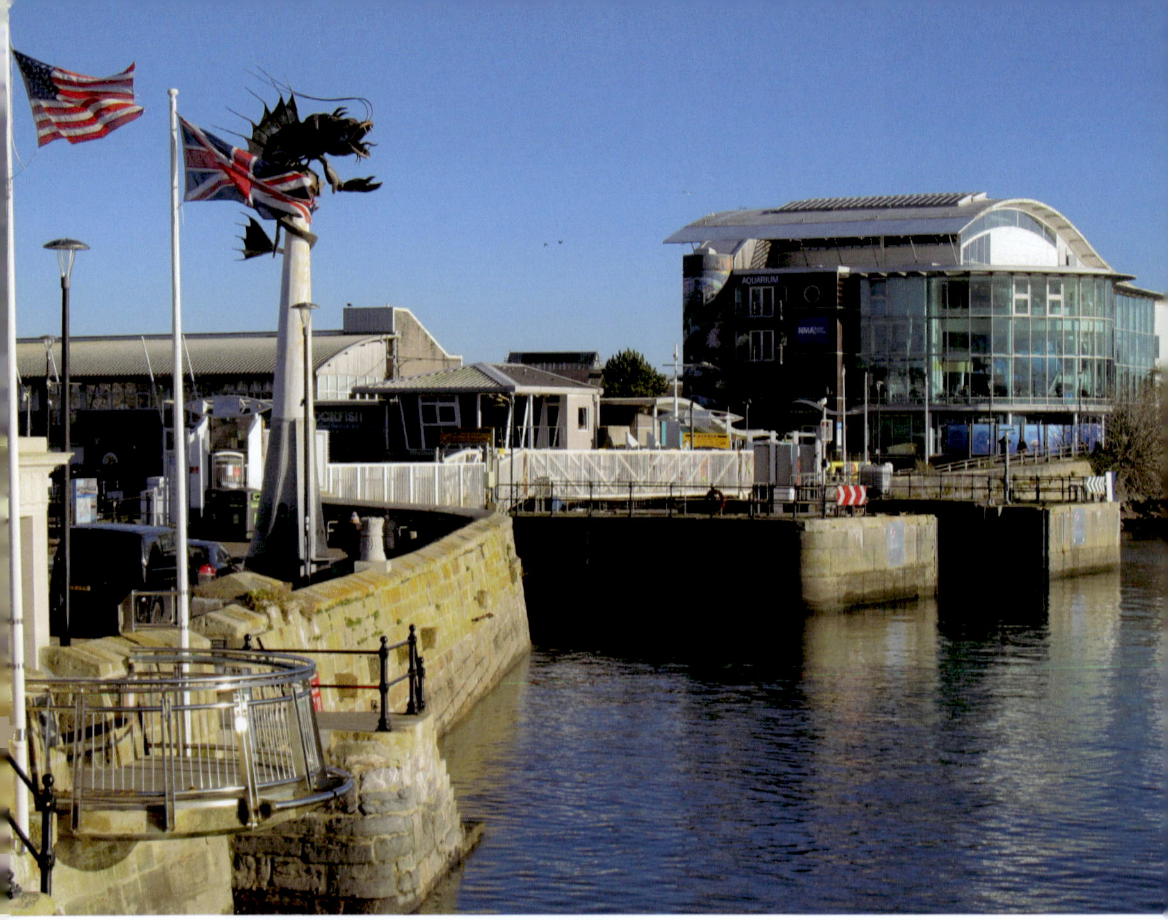

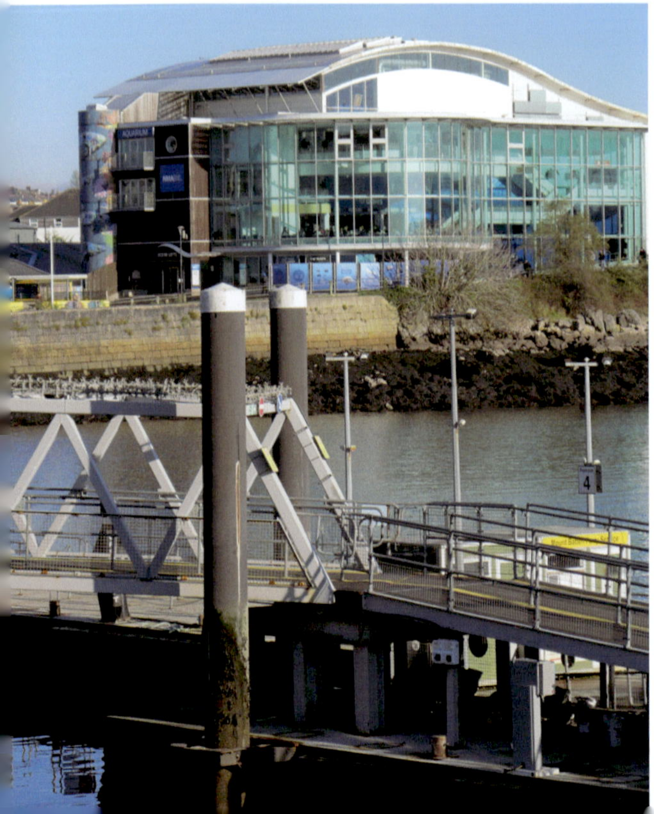

Above: A view of the National Marine Aquarium showing the *Leviathan* sculpture.

Left: Looking towards the National Marine Aquarium from across the harbour.

The aquarium is home to over 4,000 different marine animals including sharks, stingrays, octopuses, jellyfish and turtles. There are over seventy sharks including more than ten different species which range greatly in size from small catfish to large Sand Tiger Sharks. The Atlantic Ocean tank holds 2.5 million litres of water and houses animals from tiny Angelfish up to large Sand Tiger Sharks. The walk around the tank can be viewed from three different angles. Beginning at the Moon Pool tunnel and leading to the Demi tunnel, creatures that can be seen along the way include Green Turtles, Lemon Sharks, Sandbar Sharks, Southern Stingrays, Nurse Sharks, Eagle Rays and Zebra Sharks.

The Great Barrier Reef tank is an Australian themed 650,000-litre reef exhibit which includes exotic fish such as the Honeycomb Whiptail Ray, Giant Grouper, Bignose Unicornfish, Raccoon Butterflyfish, Guinea Fowl Pufferfish, Moorish Idol, Orange-lined Triggerfish, Eagle Ray, Lionfish and many other tropical species.

The Biozone area is home to colourful species from warmer climes and features the Regal Blue Tang, Triggerfish, Flame Angelfish, Bicolour Goatfish, Dot Dash Butterflyfish and Emperor Angelfish.

The Eddystone Reef exhibit features creatures found along the British coast including Sharks, Rays and Bass.

Every year, over 300,000 people visit the tourist attraction, the largest aquarium in the UK. There are daily talks and shows. As well as being a visitors' centre, the aquarium carries out ocean conservation work. Sleepover events are organised for children, scouts and families and the summer Sleepover with Sharks events prove very popular.

The proceeds from the aquarium go to a charity, the Ocean Conservation Trust.

13. The Citadel

Work began on the Citadel in 1665 after Charles II recognised Plymouth's important position as a channel port. It was built to defend the coastline from the Dutch. The building was designed by Sir Bernard de Gomme and incorporated an old fort that had been built in the time of Sir Francis Drake. Parts of the earlier Tudor fort were incorporated into the new building whose foundation stone was laid by John Granville on 18 July 1666. This stone, inscribed 'Jo Earle of Bathe 1666', is still clearly visible in the wall facing the Hoe.

When complete, the cannons not only faced towards the sea but also towards the town. This was thought to have been to keep the town in order as it had supported the parliamentarians during the Civil War in the reign of Charles' father, Charles I.

The Citadel is built of locally sourced limestone and the English baroque gateway, which was designed by Sir Thomas Fitz, is made of Portland stone. The gateway originally had a drawbridge over a dry moat, but was removed during the 1880s.

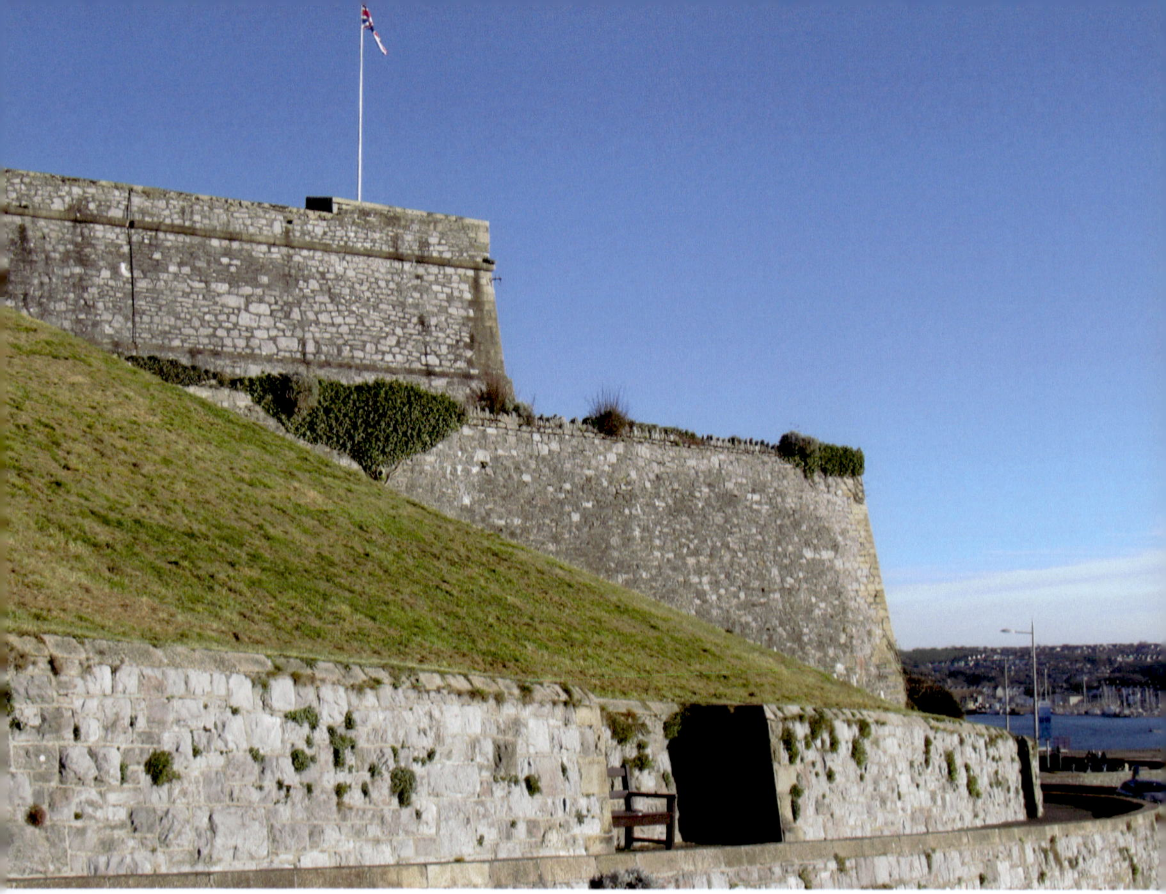

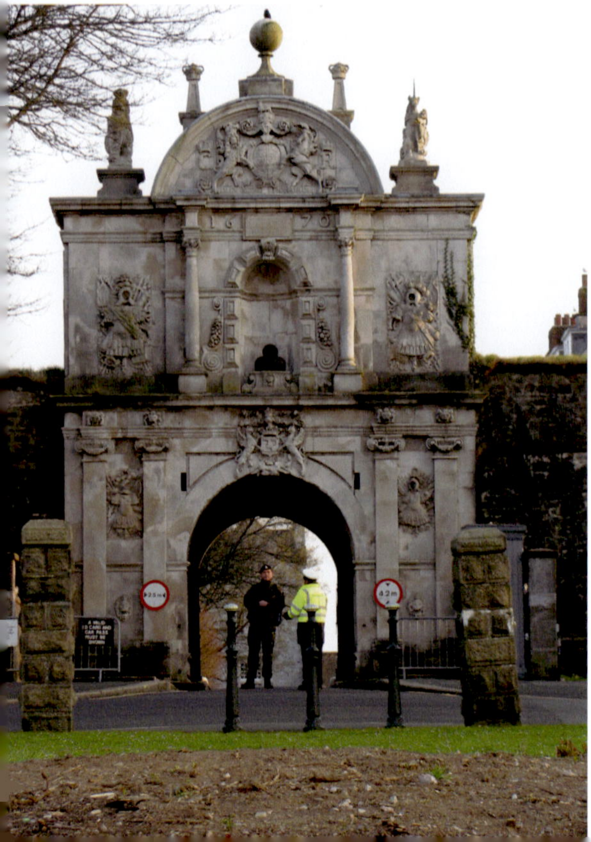

Above: The walls of the Citadel looking towards the Barbican.

Left: The entrance to the Citadel.

The Citadel is a Scheduled Monument and many of the buildings within are Grade II listed. The Citadel is thought to stand on land where the chalk giants Gog and Magog were once cut into the soil. There is a record of the chalk cut giant being on Plymouth Hoe in 1486 and a record in the City Archive shows a receipt for a bill for cleaning and weeding the giant. The bill was paid by the Earl of Edgcumbe. It is uncertain when the figure first appeared. Town records from 1486 onwards call the figure Gogmagog but in Carew's Survey of Cornwall in 1602, he refers to there being two figures on the slopes of the Hoe, both wielding clubs. One was bigger than the other and he calls them Gog and Magog, splitting the name into two halves. Several years later though, the smaller figure was being referred to as Corineus so the figures obviously commemorated an earlier wrestling match mentioned by Geoffrey of Monmouth in 1136.

14. Tinside Lido

The lido was designed by S. Wibberley, a city engineer who also designed the surrounding buildings built into the cliffside. It featured a classic semicircle pool with three fountains cascading water into the pool. The water was drawn from the sea and pumped through the cascades to give a complete change of water every four hours.

The lido was officially opened on 2 October 1935 by the Lord Mayor, Lieutenant-Commander E. W. Rogers. The three fountains were floodlit at night and gave three different colour changes.

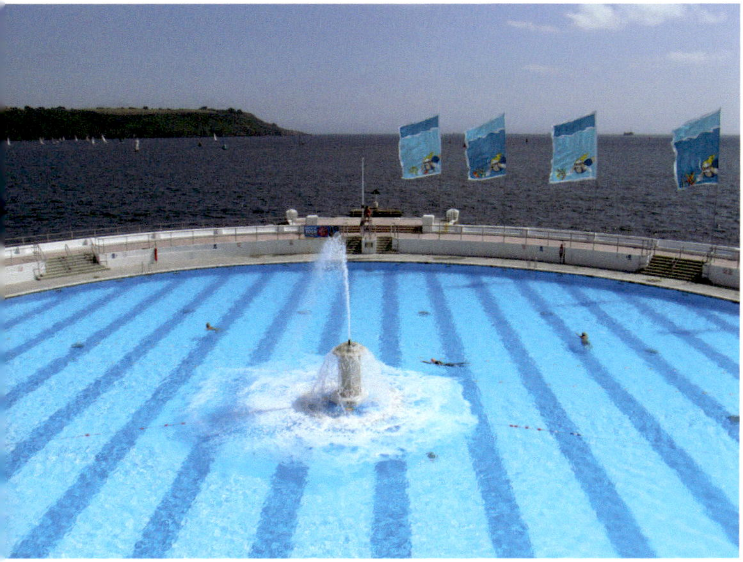

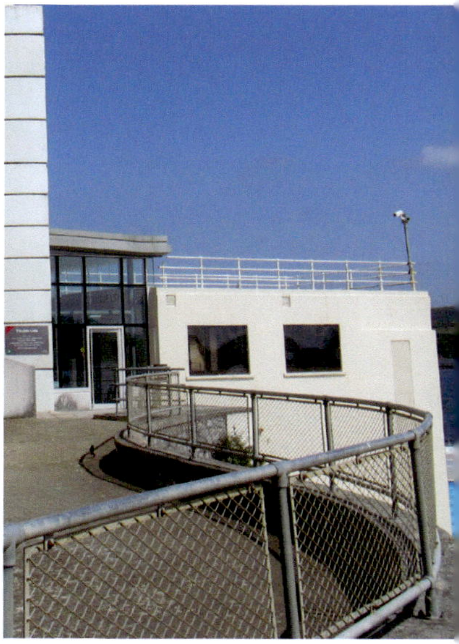

Above left: The beautiful clear water of the Lido looking towards Plymouth Sound.

Above right: The Lido main building and entrance.

Art deco in style, in it's heyday, it would have been a glorious sight. It was described in 1935 as 'one of the finest open-sea bathing centres in the country'. Orchestras played above in the terraces as people swam.

It was also once a popular venue for beauty contests. One of the things that made the lido so popular was the interest then in the new continental activity – sunbathing. This must have seemed very modern at a time when people still went to the beach dressed in their Sunday best and many men's idea of sunbathing would be to take off their thick jackets, roll their sleeves up and place a knotted hanky on their heads.

During the war years, people used the lido to wash in after spending hours clearing up the bomb-ravaged streets of Plymouth. Unfortunately, the distinctive shape of the pool helped German bombers get their bearings as they flew towards the city during many of their raids.

In the 1960s and 1970s, thousands visited the packed pool and lines of deckchairs stretched along the promenade. By the 1990s, interest in the pool had waned. It fell into disrepair and was finally closed in 1992. However, a local campaign to save it led to its renovation at a cost of £3.4 million. It became Grade II listed in 1998. The pool was reopened after completion of the work in 2005. By this time, three tidal pools, the pontoons and diving boards had been removed. It looks glorious in the summer months but has never regained the popularity that it once had.

15. The Marine Biological Association Building

The Marine Biological Association was founded in 1884 and has been based in Plymouth since 1888 when their building on Citadel Hill was first opened. The site was offered by the War Department and was thought to be ideal because of the access to salt water.

Work on the building began in 1887 and was opened on 30 January 1888 by Professor W. H. Flower, who was the director of the Natural History Museum as well as the president of the Zoological Society. Also at the event was Sir James Clarke Lawrence, the Prime Warden of the Fishmongers' Company. He had previously held the position of Lord Mayor of London. Also at the ceremony was Robert Bayly and John Bayly of Plymouth, who were both governors of the Association. After the opening, lunch was held at the Grand Hotel.

On the ground floor, a tank room became the first Plymouth Aquarium in 1888. Underground reservoirs contained almost 100,000 gallons of seawater. Originally, entry to the aquarium was free during weekdays and bank holidays. As its popularity increased an entry fee was introduced. Entry was always free to fishermen.

Constructed of Devon limestone, the building was badly damaged during the Second World War. The building was eventually repaired and the aquarium reopened to the public. The aquarium was reopened by Isaac Foot, the Lord Mayor of Plymouth, on 5 November 1946.

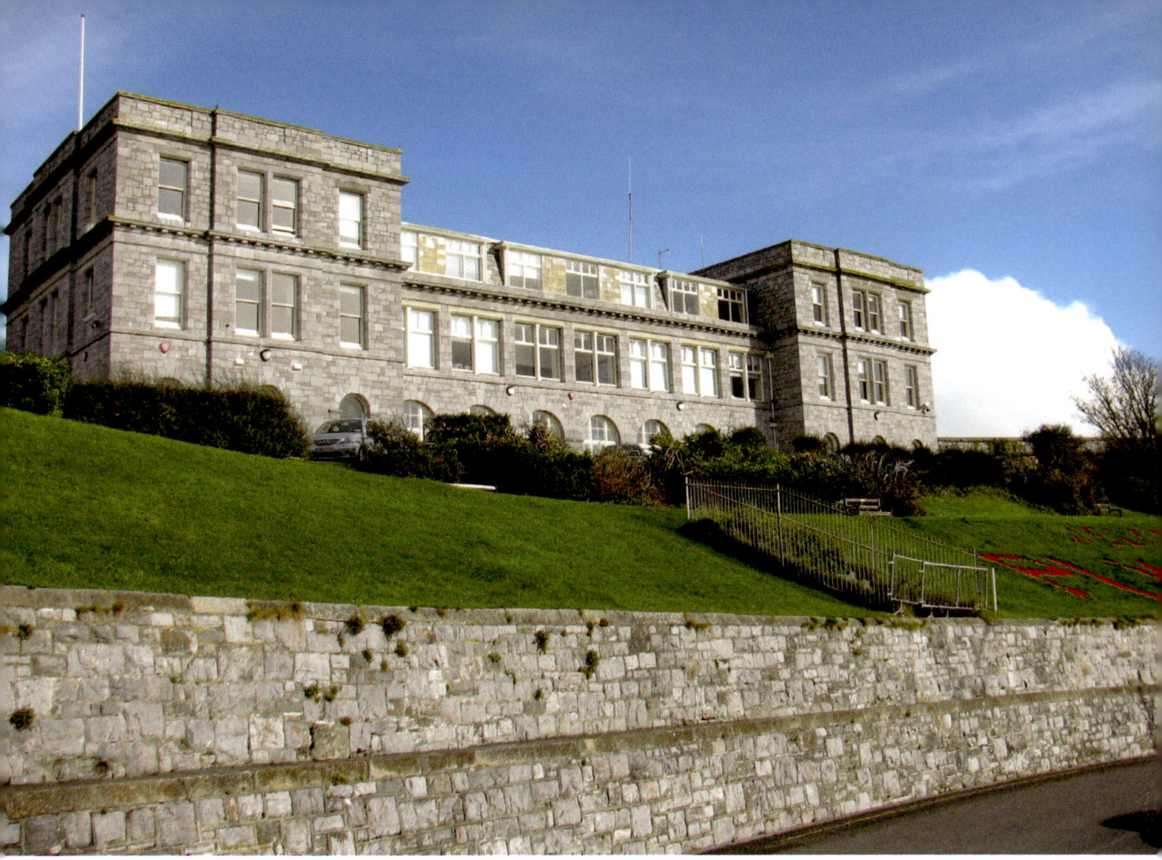

Above: The Marine Biological Association building on Plymouth Hoe.

Right: Looking towards the Marine Biological Association building. The Terrace Café can be seen on the left.

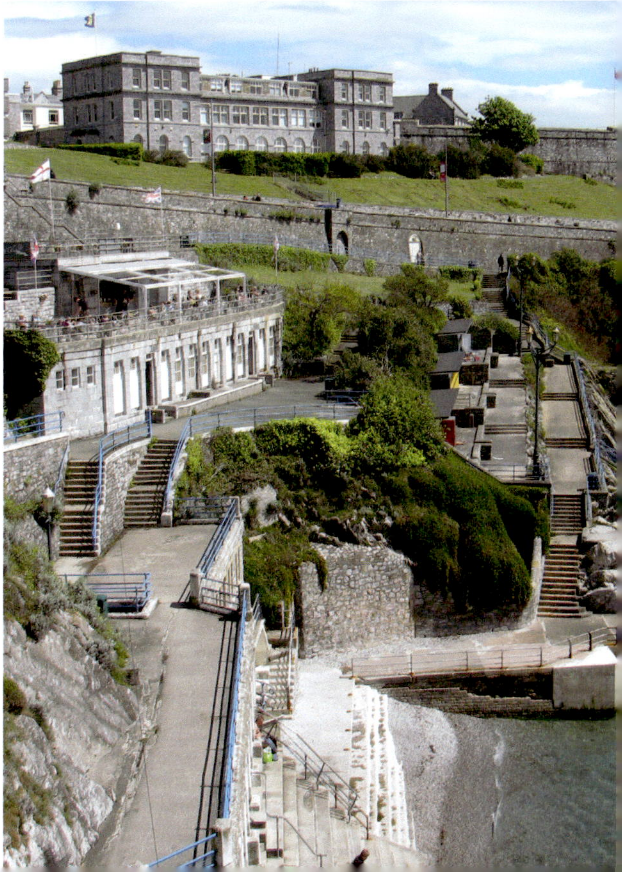

New specimens for the aquarium were collected by the association's own fishing boat, the *Sabella*, which was skippered by Captain W. J. Creese. Other exhibits were collected by the crew of the motorboat *Gammarus*, which was skippered by William Searle.

As the aquarium became more popular, it was redesigned and improved before opening again in June 1959. The building includes a scientific laboratory, as well as being home to the National Marine Biological Library. The aquarium closed when the National Marine Aquarium opened at Sutton Harbour in 1998.

16. Smeaton's Tower

Smeaton's Tower, a key landmark on Plymouth Hoe, was built by John Smeaton on the Eddystone Reef in 1759. There had been two previous lighthouses on the reef. The first was built by Henry Winstanley in 1695. However, seven years later, during a storm, it was washed away taking its builder with it.

The second lighthouse was built in 1711 by John Rudyerd but was destroyed by a fire in 1755. Work commenced on Smeaton's Tower in December 1756 to

Smeaton's Tower on Plymouth Hoe. Sir Francis Drake's statue can be seen in the background.

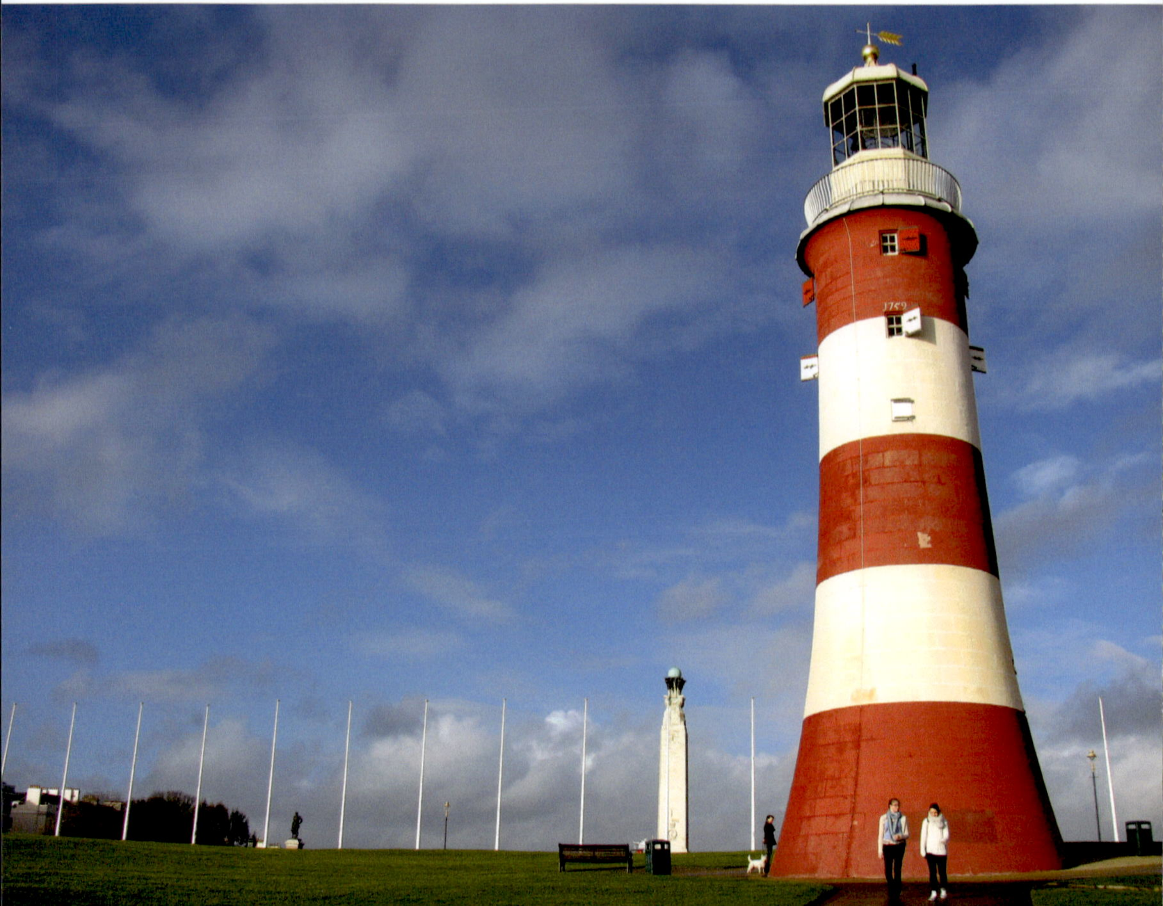

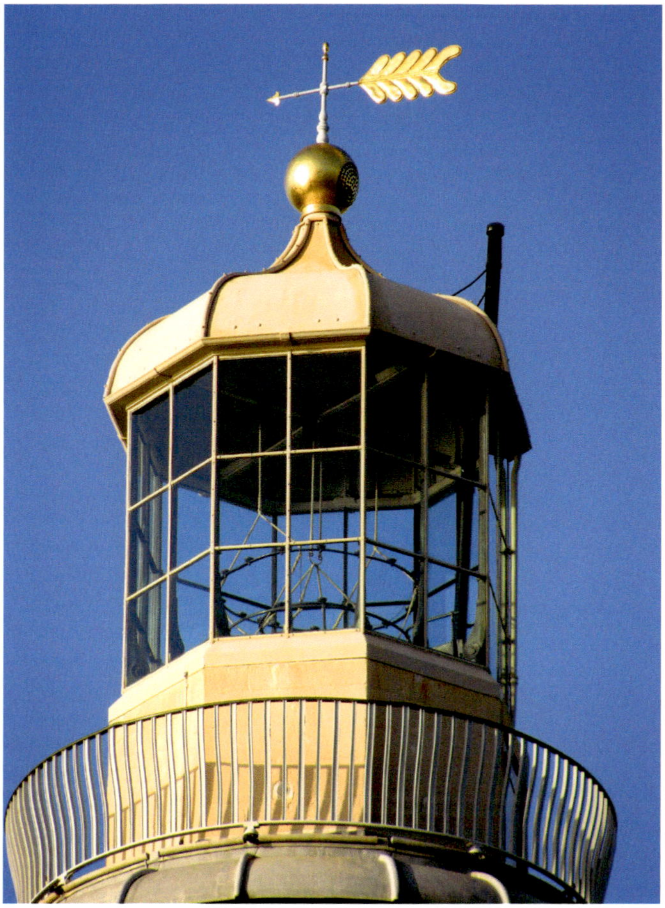

The old lantern housing and viewing platform at the top of Smeaton's Tower.

replace the damaged lighthouse. Smeaton's Tower would still be there today but the rock underneath it was undermined by the sea. James Douglass built a new lighthouse on an adjoining rock. It was felt that if Smeaton's Tower was left standing beside the new lighthouse, that it could eventually collapse onto the new lighthouse if the rock beneath it became even more undermined. It was decided to blow it up but Mr F. J. Webb suggested that it should be dismantled and erected on the Hoe where the Trinity House Navigational Obelisk once stood. This was quite a task and the lighthouse was removed stone by stone and rebuilt on the Hoe with a new base to support it. The original base can still be seen, out to sea, beside the present Eddystone Lighthouse. On 24 September 1884, the Lord Mayor opened Smeaton's Tower to the public.

In 1913, a bomb was planted at Smeaton's Tower by suffragettes. The story was reported in *The Western Times*, which stated that a serious explosion would have occurred if the fuse had not burnt out. While passing the tower, a man named William Chubb found a 6-inch-long circular canister in the doorway which contained half a pound of powder. In the cover was a wick saturated with paraffin oil, which had evidently been lighted but had been blown out by the wind. Painted in crude letters in black paint on the tin were the words 'Votes for Women! Death in Ten Minutes!'

Today, the tower is painted in its original red and white colour scheme.

17. The Dome

The Dome, facing Plymouth Sound, was built in 1988 and opened the following year. Previously, the Mallard Café (named after the Mallard buoy) stood on the same piece of land. The café was opened in 1965 and proved very popular with its spectacular views over Plymouth Sound. It was removed in the 1980s in preparation for the building of the Dome.

The Dome was originally built as a small museum and tourist information centre and was designed by architect Tony Irish. It featured a collection of themed galleries that covered the history of Plymouth. It also had two observation galleries that overlooked Plymouth Sound. A huge globe of the world was displayed in the main part. The idea for the building was conceived as part of the Mayflower celebrations and was visited by Queen Elizabeth II on 20 July 1988. At the same time, she unveiled a plaque that commemorated the 400th anniversary of the

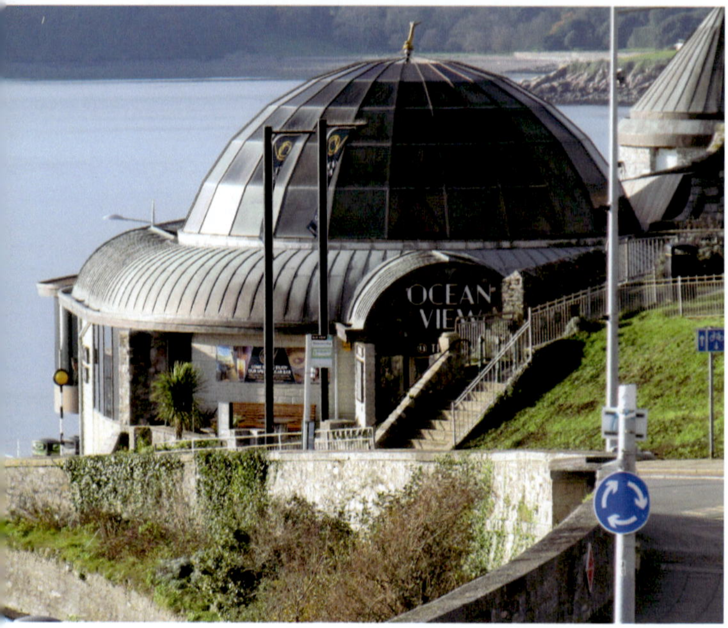

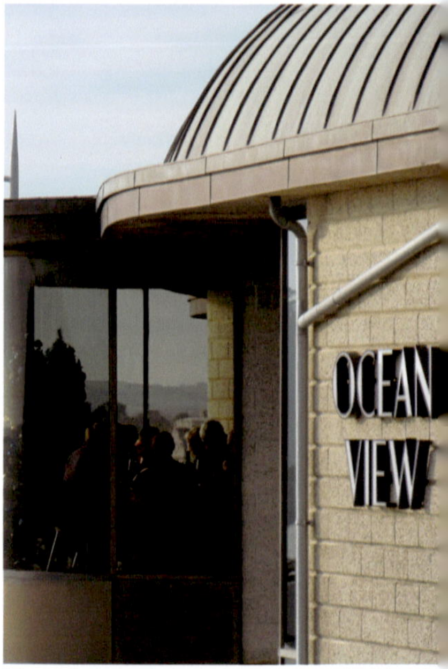

Above left: Looking towards the Dome with Plymouth Sound in the background.

Above right: A view of the diners within the Ocean View restaurant at the Dome.

battle with the Spanish Armada in 1588. The museum and tourist information centre were closed in 2006.

Celebrity chef Gary Rhodes opened a restaurant within the Dome in 2013, which closed in 2016. Today, the building houses the art deco Ocean View Bar and Restaurant.

18. No. 3 Elliot Terrace

Elliot Terrace was built in 1860 by John Pethick. In 1908, No. 3 Elliot Terrace was bought by Waldorf Astor, who had come to Plymouth as a Unionist Parliamentary candidate before, later, becoming Mayor of Plymouth between 1939 and 1944. His wife Nancy gave No. 3 Elliot Terrace to the city as a residence for future lord mayors.

Nancy Witcher Langhorne (later Nancy Astor) was born in Virginia in 1879 and moved to England at the age of twenty-six where she married Waldorf Astor.

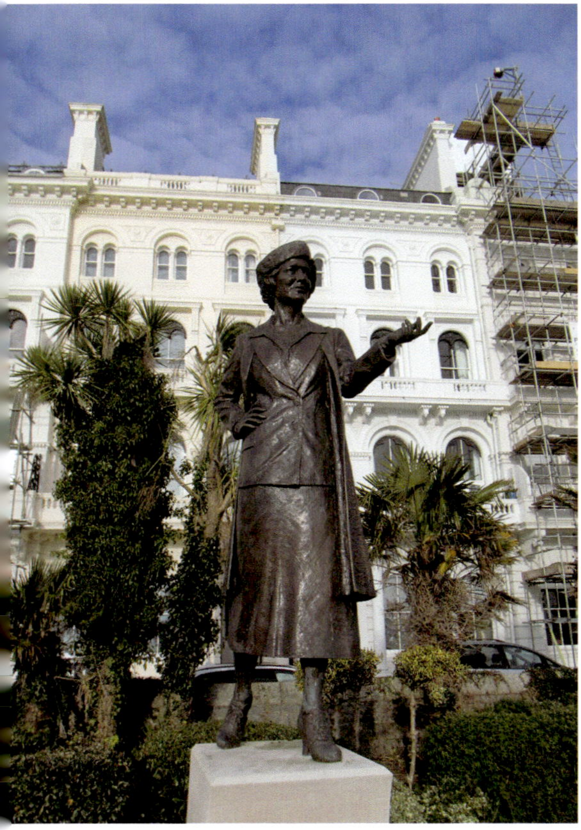

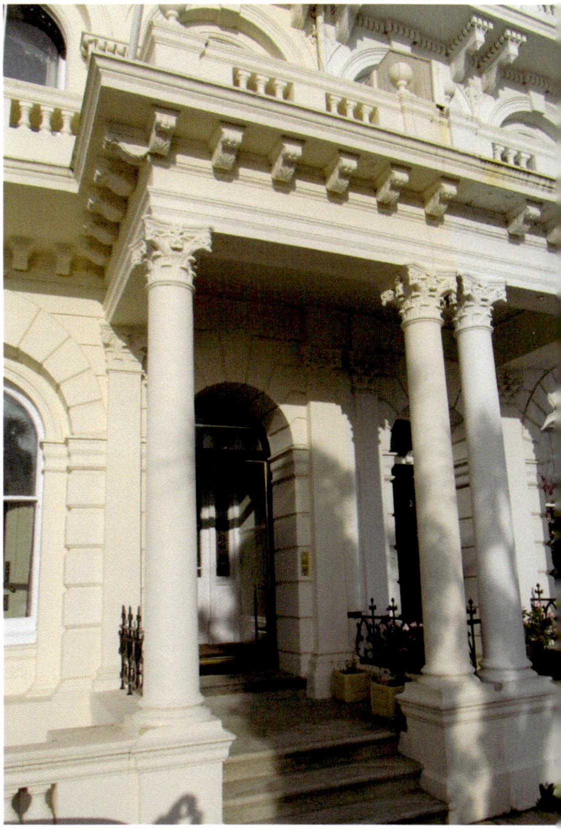

Above left: Nancy Astor's statue in front of her old home at No. 3 Elliot Terrace.

Above right: The ornate entrance to No. 3 Elliot Terrace.

She entered politics soon after and won her husband's former seat in Plymouth in 1919, becoming the first woman MP to sit in the House of Commons.

During the Second World War, Nancy Astor was Lady Mayoress of Plymouth, living on the Hoe at No. 3 Elliot Terrace. Regular visitors included Charlie Chaplin, George Bernard Shaw and Amy Johnson.

Al fresco dancing on the Hoe began during the first week of May 1941 and was a success from the beginning. The idea was first suggested by Lord Astor. Lady Astor regularly took part in the gatherings and among her dancing partners was the Duke of Kent. During the war years, the dancing raised people's spirits and brought everyone together.

Noel Coward, a friend of the Astors, said at the time, 'After all that devastation, on a Summer evening, people were dancing on the Hoe. It made me cry – the bravery, the gallantry, the Englishness of it!' A huge dance was held on the Hoe at the end of the war to celebrate VE Day.

Lady Astor was well-known for her straight to the point way of talking. She once said to Winston Churchill, 'If I was your wife I would give you poison!', to which Churchill replied, 'If I was your husband, I'd drink it!' Lady Astor died in 1964.

No. 3 Elliot Terrace is still the Lord Mayor's residence and is licenced for civil ceremonies. The house can be hired for the day and is filled with artifacts, photos and antiques from Nancy Astor's time there. There are also regular tours.

19. The Grand Hotel

The Grand Hotel was built by John Pethick, who was a respected builder and later mayor of the city between 1898 and 1900. He also provided the base for Smeaton's Tower when it was rebuilt on the Hoe. Petherick was known as Honest John and when the building was completed in 1879, he became its first owner. The building features stucco finish with stucco detail together with a dry slate mansard roof over a moulded eaves cornice and has an Italianate influence.

When it was built, the Grand was the only hotel in Plymouth with a sea view and adverts stated that it had the finest views in Europe. In 1889, eighty-year-old Prime Minister William Ewart Gladstone addressed a crowd of 100,000 from the balcony.

Oliver Hardy stayed there for a short while. He had a severe bout of the flu and also had a mild heart attack while appearing at the New Palace Theatre in a production of *Birds of a Feather* on 17 May 1954. The show was cancelled and Hardy spent the rest of his stay in Plymouth recovering at the Grand Hotel before returning to America on a cruise liner.

In 1963, the Berni company bought the hotel for £100,000 and spent £60,000 modernising it. Their priority was providing reasonably priced food and so ten bedrooms were removed and four new restaurants were added.

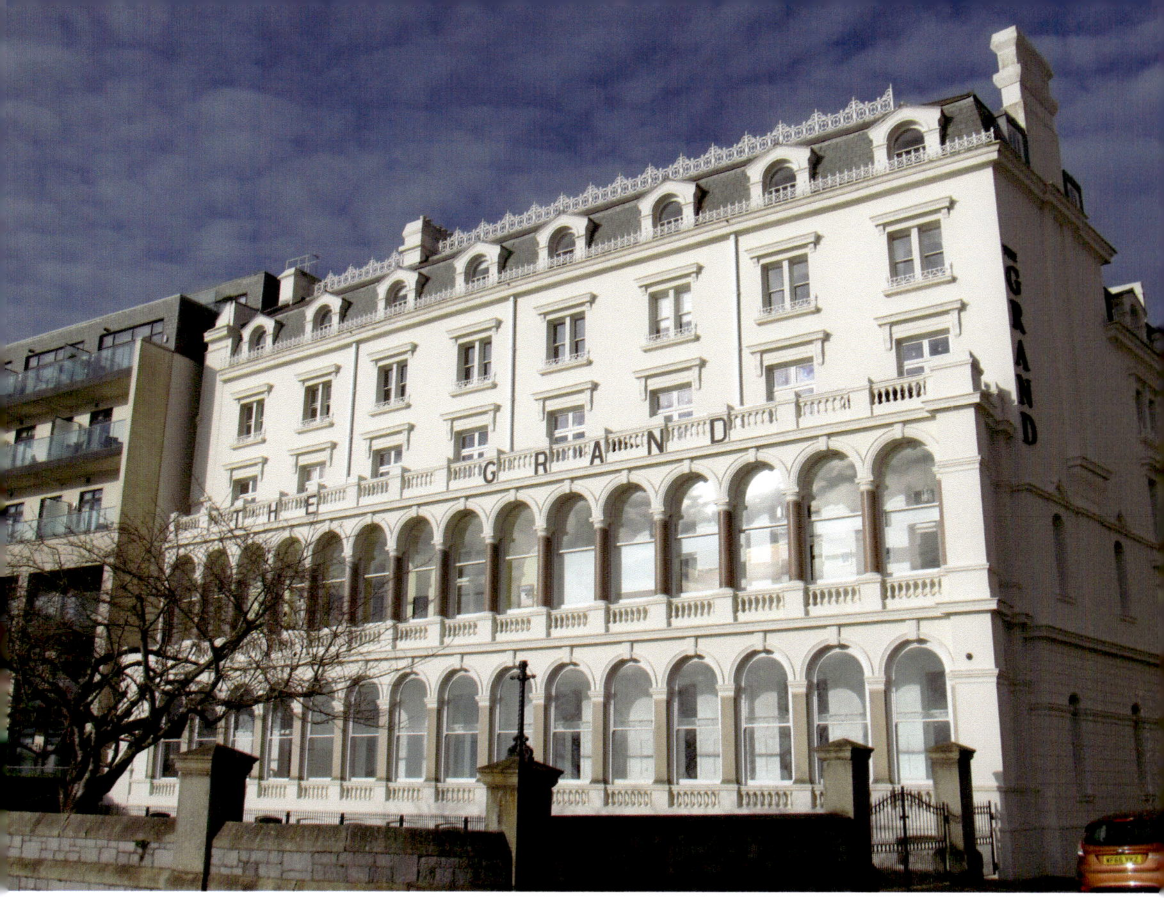

Above: The Grand Hotel on Plymouth Hoe.

Right: The stylish windows and balconies of the Grand Hotel.

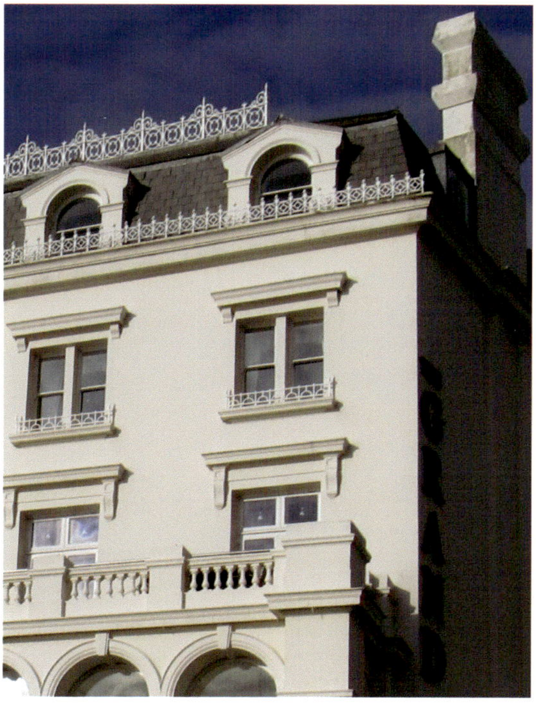

The Beatles stopped there for lunch in September 1967 while filming *Magical Mystery Tour*. The Beatles signed autographs in Elliot Street in front of the Grand before having their photos taken sitting on the Hoe slopes with Smeaton's Tower in the background. The Berni Grand proved very popular for many years with Plymouth families before being sold in 1985.

After the hotel was affected by fire in 2003, it was refurbished as part of a redevelopment plan by Devington Homes at a cost of £12 million. It features twenty-two apartments and four penthouses and many original features have been retained or refurbished.

The building is Grade II listed.

20. The Duke of Cornwall Hotel

The Duke of Cornwall Hotel was opened opposite Millbay station in 1865 to cater for the many rail passengers who travelled onwards by train or on one of the many passenger liners that docked regularly. The first steam train arrived on 2 April 1849. The arrival of the railways was a great boost to the Three Towns allowing passengers to travel to London in nine hours. Previously, the journey had taken over twenty-one hours taking a horse-drawn coach.

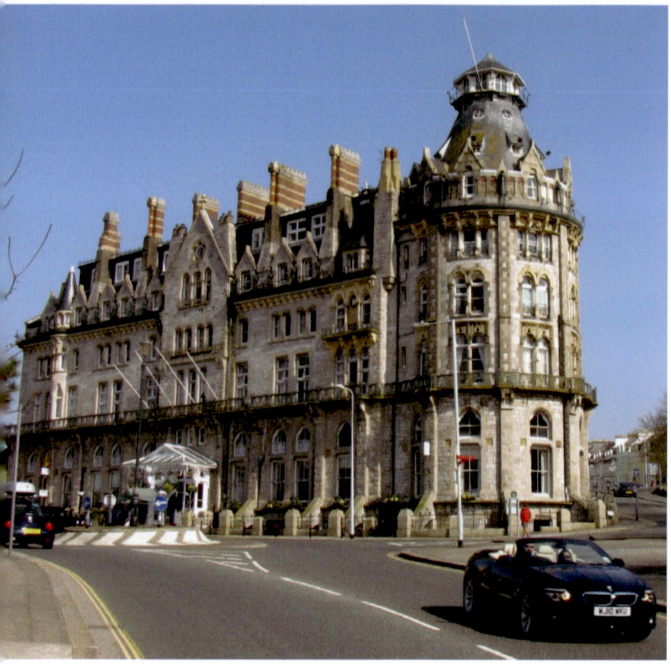

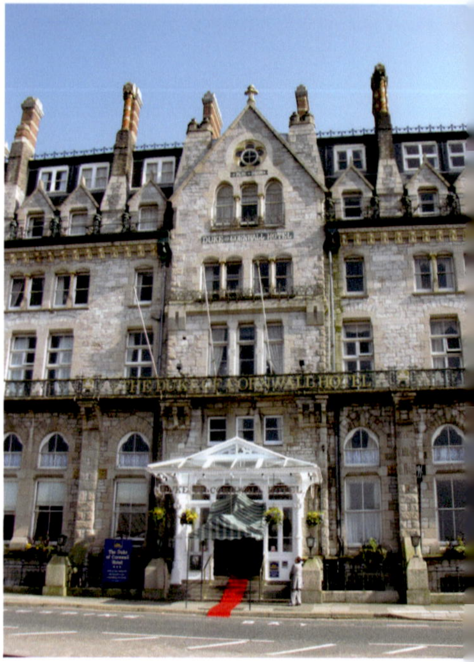

Above left: The impressive Duke of Cornwall Hotel building.

Above right: The entrance to the Duke of Cornwall Hotel complete with red carpet.

The hotel was designed by Charles Hayward and the building work was carried out by Messrs Hall and Pethick at a cost of £40,000. John Pethick was responsible for constructing many of Plymouth's fine buildings. Construction began in 1863 and the hotel's structure contained five different types of stone. It was built in a Victorian Gothic style. The area had to be first excavated to clear the large site where the Saracens Head public house and Millbay Grove Terrace had once stood.

In 1912, the hotel hosted twenty stewardesses who had survived the sinking of the RMS *Titanic*. By the 1920s, road travel had increased greatly. Liners arriving in Plymouth grew from 350 to over 750 a year. This increased the need for extra accommodation. Liner passengers realised that by disembarking at Plymouth they could save a whole day getting back to London by continuing on by train instead of staying onboard to its destination in Southampton. The spare day led to people looking for accommodation and because of this the Duke of Cornwall Hotel was refurbished and had electric lighting fitted and a lift installed.

Amongst the many famous guests over the years was Ernest Shackleton, who stayed at the hotel in 1914 prior to embarking on his Imperial Trans-Antarctic Expedition.

The Duke of Cornwall Hotel narrowly escaped bombing in the Second World War and remains much the same today. In the 1970s and early 1980s, the hotel faced closure but it was saved by a major refurbishment after the poet Sir John Betjeman praised its architecture.

21. Plymouth Pavilions

Plymouth Pavilions opened in 1991 as an entertainment and leisure centre. The arena within the building has the capacity to hold 4,000 standing, 2,500 seated. The complex once included a well-used pool but this closed in 2012 when the Plymouth Life Centre opened at Central Park. The facility also has an ice rink.

Originally, the land housed the once very busy Millbay station, which was a casualty of the Second World War. It first opened in 1849 and remained in service for many years. It was bombed in 1941 and was closed to passengers shortly afterwards. For many years afterwards, it was known by locals as 'The Shabby Shed'. It was cleared away in the 1970s and the large area of land was used as a car park and also as an open-air market, a continuation of the market that once operated on the land now occupied by the Toys R Us building. In the late 1970s, two large inflatable domes were erected on the land and these hosted exhibitions, talks and shows. They survived until the early 1980s.

Pillars from the original Millbay station still stand by the Pavilions building. The railway bridge leading towards Millbay station was removed in the 1970s.

World renowned architect David Mackay suggested in 2003 the Pavilions should be knocked down to improve access from the city centre to the sea as part

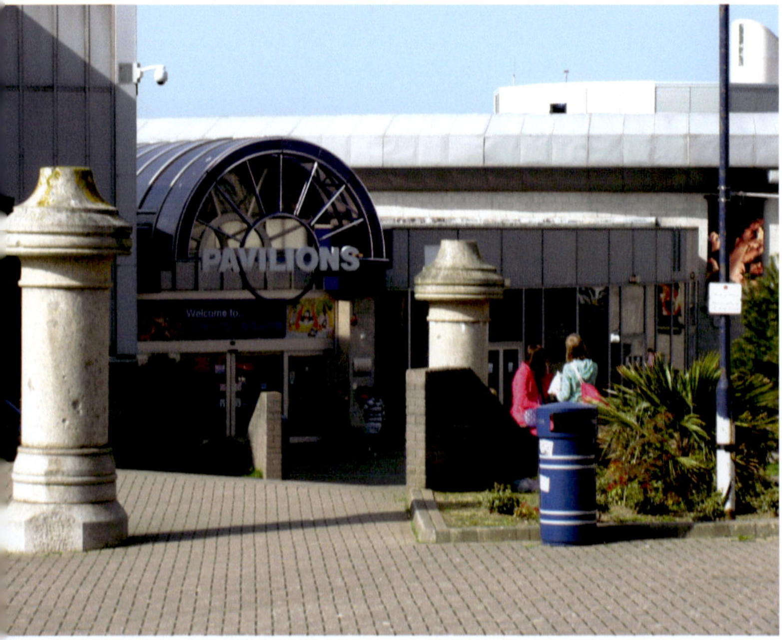

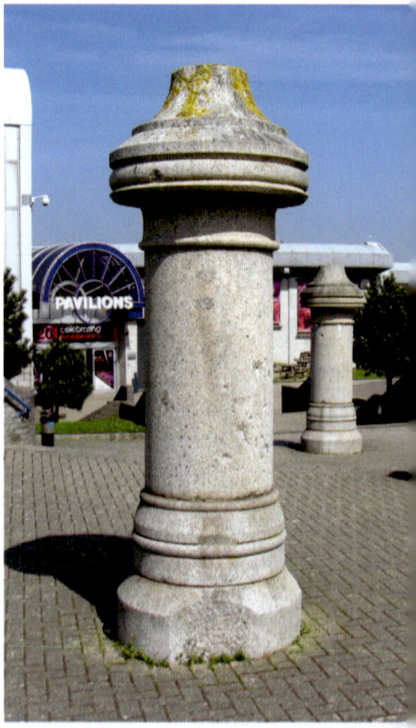

Above left: The entrance to Plymouth Pavilions.

Above right: The posts outside the Plymouth Pavilions building, which were once part of Millbay station. Shrapnel marks from the Second World War can be seen on their sides.

of a proposal to construct a broad avenue from Western Approach down to the sea, which he felt would give the city more of a metropolitan feel. Whilst a similar plan is underway, so far the Plymouth Pavilions building still remains.

22. The ABC Cinema

The Theatre Royal and adjoining Royal Hotel in George Street were designed by John Foulston and George Wightwick and opened in August 1813. Although magnificent buildings, they were demolished in 1937 to make way for a purpose-built cinema, the Royal, which later became the ABC in 1958.

The cinema was built in an art deco design and was designed by in-house architect W. R. Glen and housed 2,024 seats. The building was faced in white Portland stone, as were many of the buildings in the city centre.

In November 1963, the Beatles played at the ABC to screaming fans so loud that their music could barely be heard. The band later stayed the night at the Burgh Island Hotel in Bigbury. They returned to the ABC the following year in October 1964.

The ABC closed temporarily in October 1976 so that the cinema could be converted into a three-screen venue together with a bingo hall. The final films shown while it was still a single screen cinema were *The Likely Lads* and *Steptoe and Son*.

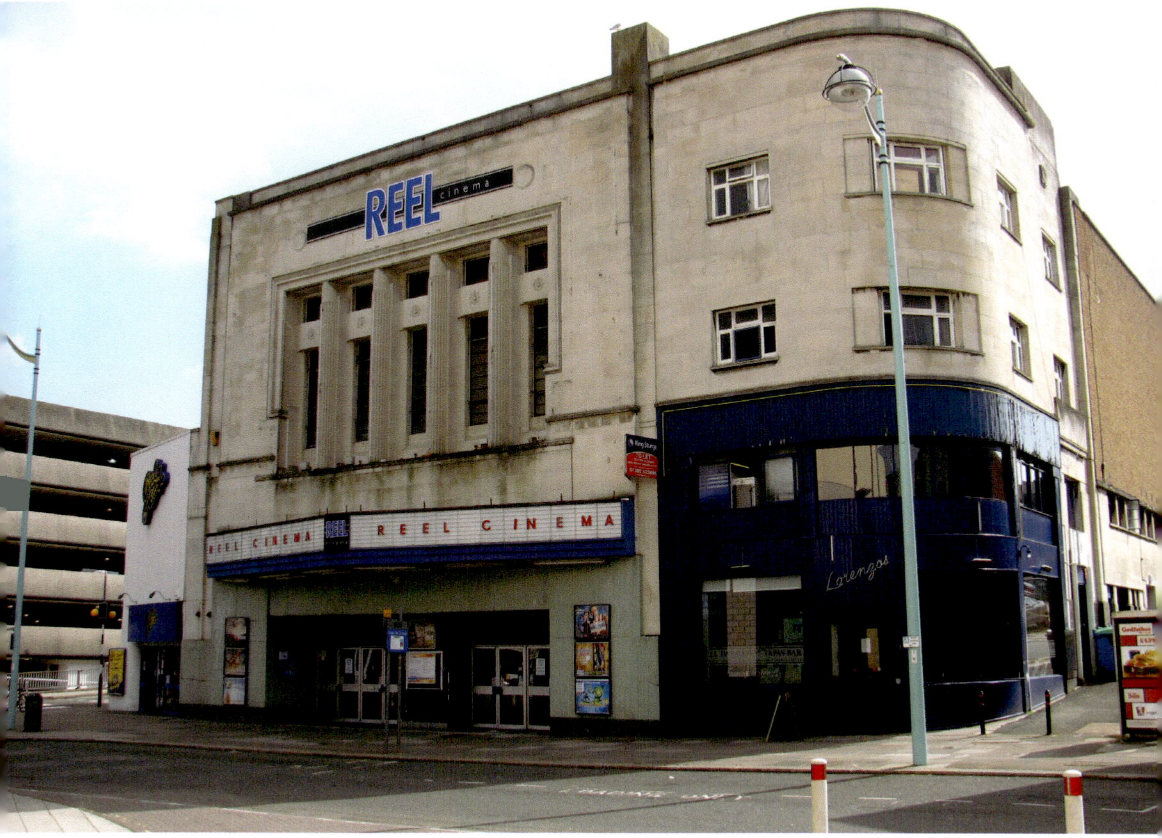

Above: The Reel Cinema before it closed. It was formerly the ABC.

Right: A view of the front of the Reel Cinema building.

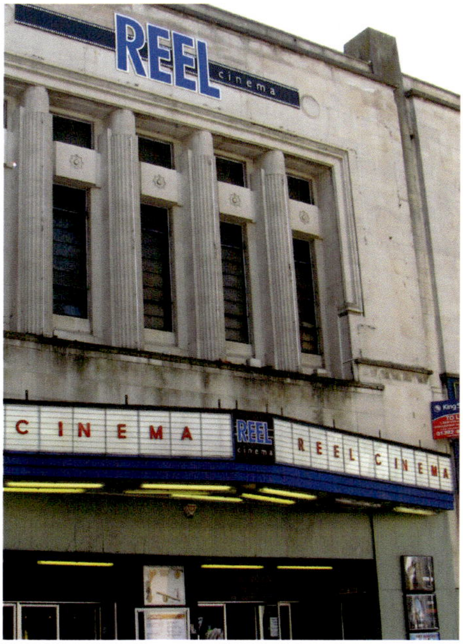

The cinema reopened in May 1977. The first movies shown were *The Enforcer* with Clint Eastwood at ABC 1, *The Sentinel* starring Chris Sarandon at ABC 2 and *The Big Bus*, an American disaster comedy film, starring Joseph Bologna in ABC 3.

In the early 1980s, cinema audiences greatly reduced with the advent of video recorders but things picked up again towards the end of the decade. In 1987, the ABC was taken over by Cannon and became the Cannon Cinema, although most locals still continued to refer to it as the ABC. Its next owners were MGM before a management buyout saw the cinema revert to its old name of the ABC in the mid-1990s. In 2006, it was bought out and became the Reel Cinema.

The cinema finally closed its doors in February 2019. For a while, it looked as if the building would be demolished but recent plans have suggested that it could reopen as a music venue.

23. Plymouth Athenaeum

The Plymouth Institute was founded in 1812 and was renamed the Plymouth Institution soon after. Their original meetings took place in Catherine Street and later at the Frankfort Street Art Gallery.

In December 1817, the Plymouth Institution decided to build an Athenaeum on land near to the Royal Hotel and Theatre in George Street. John Foulston became

The Athenaeum building. Westward Studios, later TSW, used to stand to its right.

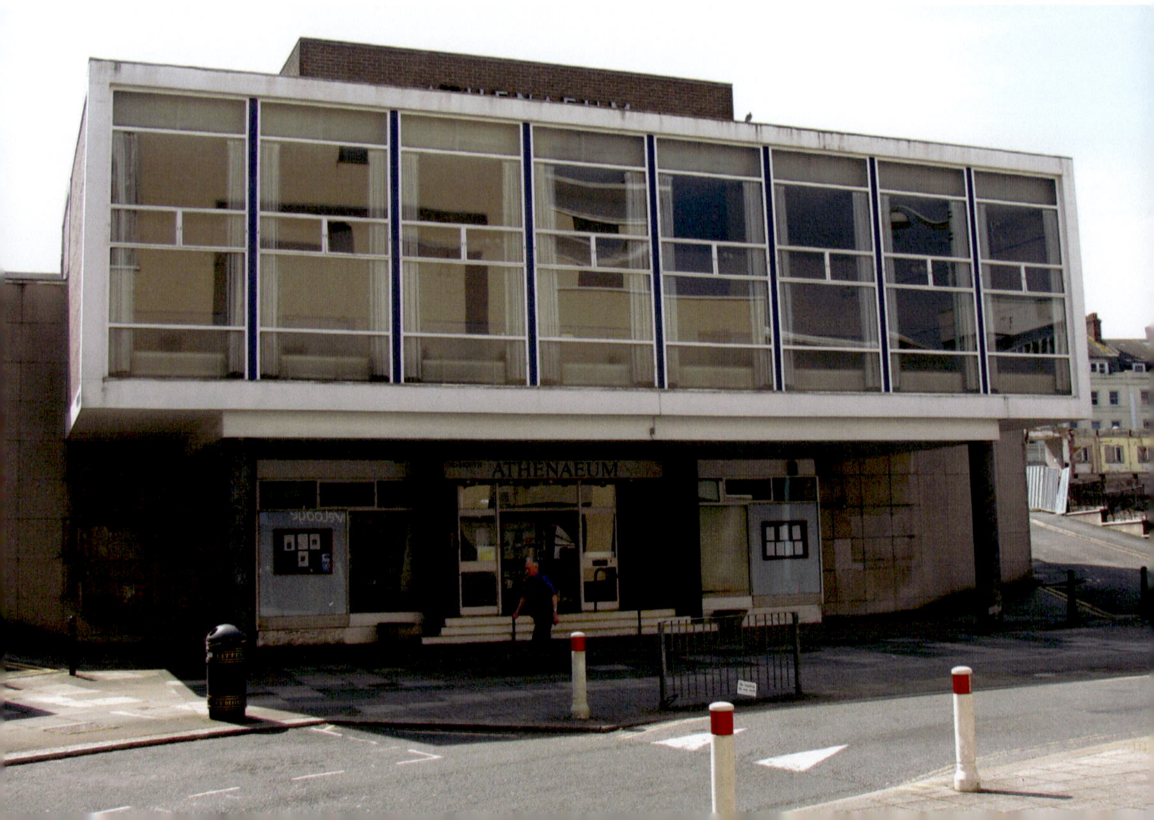

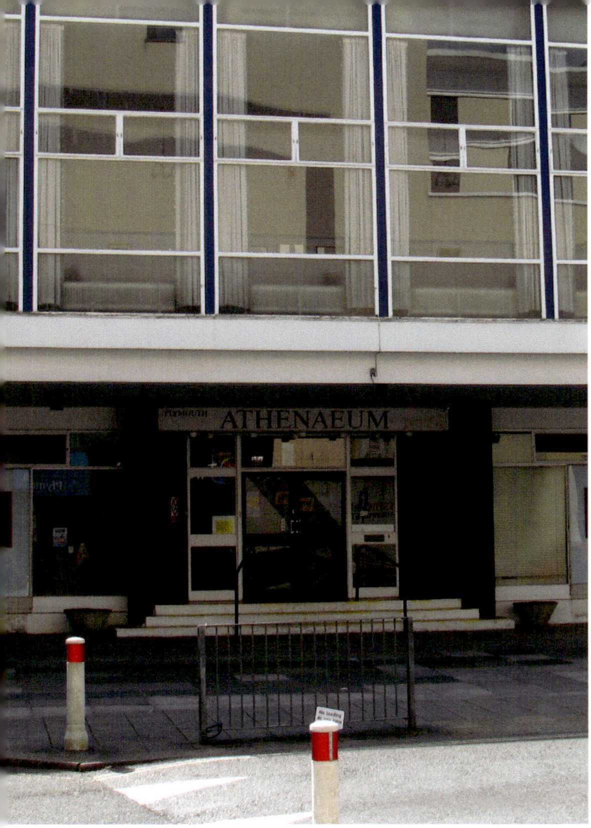

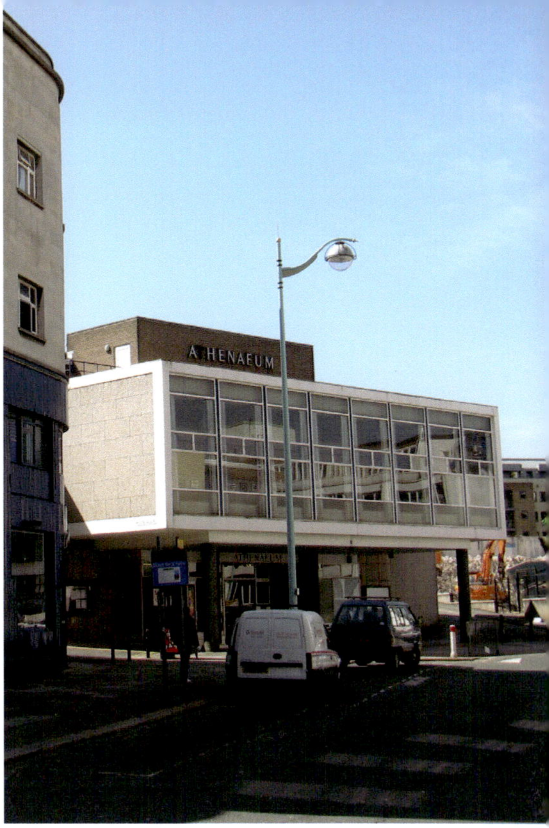

Above left: The entrance to the Athenaeum building.

Above right: Looking towards the Athenaeum building. The cleared land where the television studio once stood can be seen in the background.

a founder member and offered his services freely to design an Athenaeum which would match the classical façades of the adjacent buildings.

The original Athenaeum constructed in 1818 featured a Greek Doric-style façade. Visitors included the architect George Wightwick and Dr Cookworthy with notable members including Charles Darwin, Isaac Foot, John Foulston and Stanley Gibbons. The museum contained many unusual exhibits including four tattooed Maori heads and the Barbican ducking chair which had last been used to punish Nancy Clark, an elderly fisherwoman, for assault and her use of bad language. In the 1800s, exhibits of Romano-British coins found at Mount Batten together with several gold nuggets went missing, presumed stolen, and the matter was recorded by a Mrs Wilson.

The building was destroyed during the Blitz of 1941. Many irreplaceable exhibits were lost forever due to the bombing including fine china, paintings, a vast library of rare books and relics from the Cattedown bone caves. The library alone had over 10,000 volumes on subjects such as science and natural history.

The new Athenaeum was built in 1961. It was opened by the Lord Mayor, Alderman Arthur Goldberg. The lost library was restored and is a full member of the Association of Independent Libraries. The current Athenaeum features a two tier auditorium and a lecture theatre. The theatre proved popular with local dancing schools and amateur dramatic groups until it closed in 2009 due to financial problems. However, after local funding, it was reopened in 2017.

The Athenaeum has a lounge which runs the length of the front of the building. It has hosted many prominent speakers over the years including broadcasters John Snagge and Edgar Lustgarten, as well as Church of England envoy Terry Waite and local artist Robert Lenkiewicz.

24. The Civic Centre

After the destruction of Plymouth in the Second World War, the Civic Centre became the final part in the process of reconstructing the city. The building was designed by city architect Hector Stirling and was inspired by the Lever Building in New York with its eye-catching glass fronted façade.

Stirling's design was approved in 1957 but parts of it were amended by architects Jellicoe, Ballantyne and Colleridge. Geoffrey Jellicoe was known for being a landscape architect. He proposed replacing the full glass frontage with a two-tone glass and concrete building together with a wing-shaped roof above the top-floor restaurant. However, Stirling's main concept and layout remained.

Excavation work began in January 1958 by Messrs Richard Costain and in August that year, Staverton Builders began the foundation and substructure work.

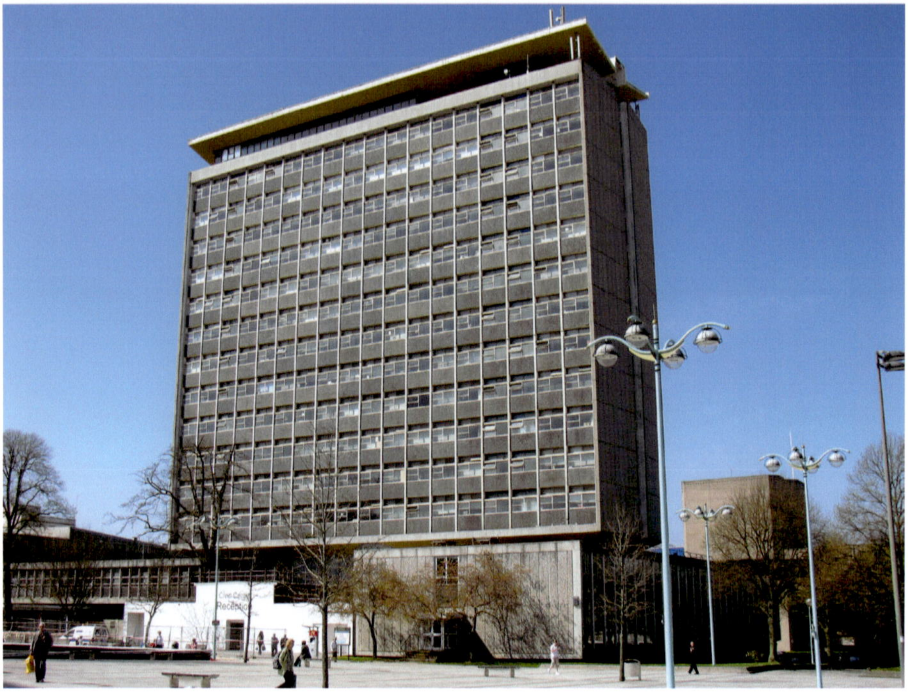

The Civic Centre building with the Theatre Royal building in the background.

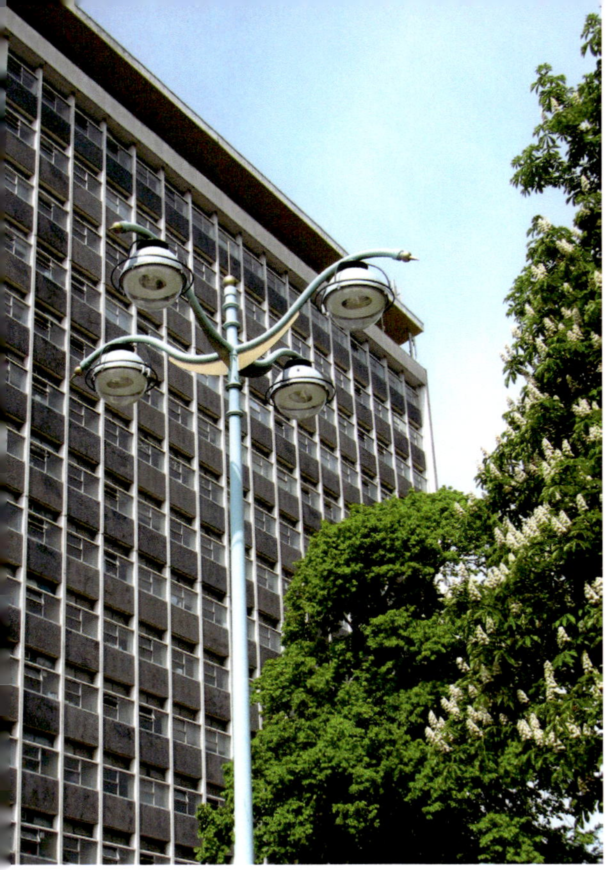

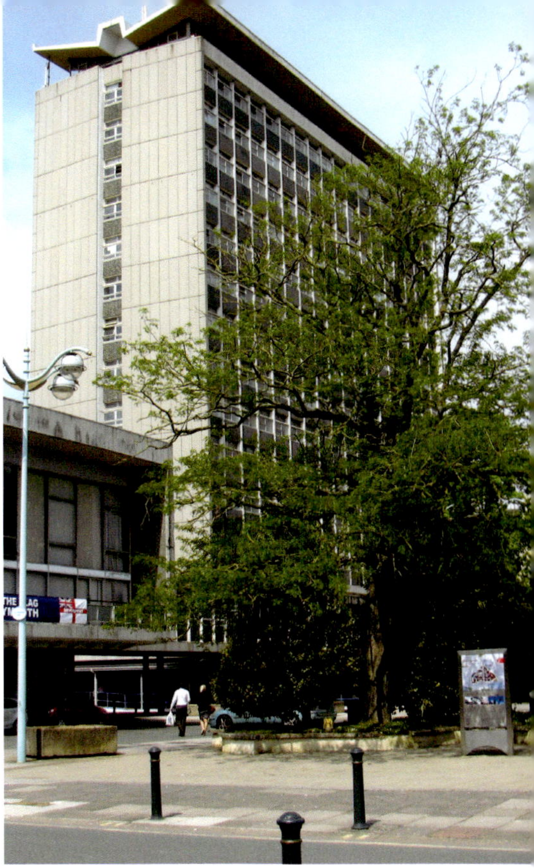

Above left: Looking up towards the fourteen-storey Civic Centre.

Above right: The Civic Centre in Armada Way. The two-storey Council House building is on the left.

Work on the adjoining Council House began in November 1959 and was carried out by Messrs Humphreys Ltd. Although there were worries considering the cost of the tower, the work was completed on time. The whole project cost £1,600,000 to build. The council moved into the building in March 1962 and the building was officially opened by Queen Elizabeth II in July that year. For the first time, the city's municipal departments were all housed in one building. Prior to the Second World War, the council had various offices scattered across the city.

It incorporated the central offices of the Plymouth City Council until it was sold in 2015. Plymouth City Council later moved to Ballard House once the home of British Telecom.

For many years, visitors could travel to the top floor of the building to visit the restaurant but this was closed in 1975. There was also access to the viewing platform, which allowed visitors views across the city and towards the Hoe and the Sound. However, this faculty was later closed.

In 2007, the building became Grade II listed, which saved it from demolition. The building was abandoned by the city council after it fell into disrepair. However, there are plans to renovate it and turn it into 144 residential apartments.

25. Plymouth Guildhall

The current Guildhall was Plymouth's fifth guildhall, the original being built in the fifteenth century and located in the Old Town. The foundation stone of the current Guildhall was laid in July 1870 by the mayor William Luscombe. The building was designed by Norman and Hine together with artistic direction by Edward William Godwin. It was built in the Gothic Revival style by Messrs Call and Pethick at a cost of £50,000. The Guildhall was completed in 1874 and officially opened by the Prince of Wales in August of that year.

The outline for the west front, which now features the building's entrance, included an octagonal tower to the left, with an 160-foot-high square tower to the right. The main room inside was the Great Hall, which included a pipe organ made by Henry Willis & Sons.

The Guildhall was almost completely destroyed by the Blitz of 1941 when only its outer shell remained. The great hall, which was 146 feet by 58 feet, was totally destroyed by the bombing of 1941 and it took another ten years to decide whether to rebuild or demolish it completely. Paton Watson and Patrick Abercombie proposed demolishing the building as part of the plan to redevelop Plymouth. However, the proposal was rejected by one vote at a council meeting in 1951. It was finally decided to rebuild it and it was reopened in 1959, some eighteen years

The Guildhall entrance from Royal Parade.

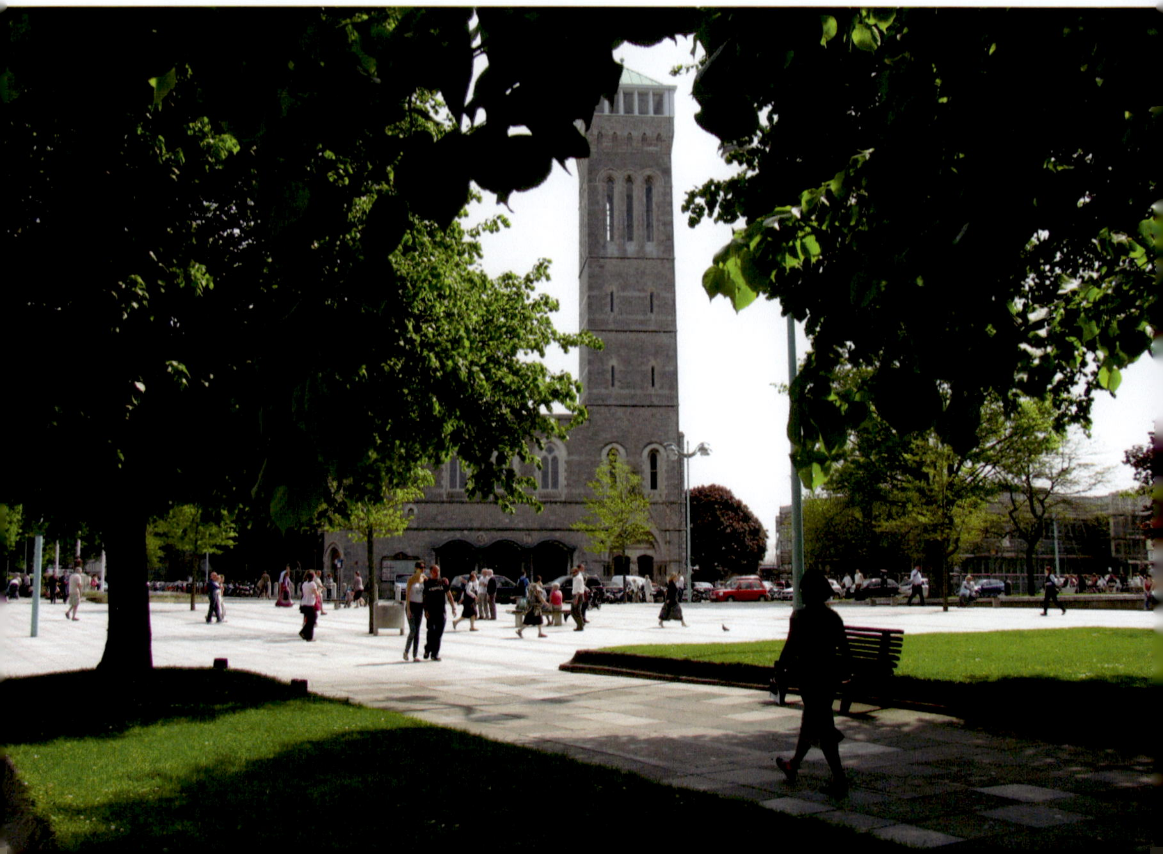

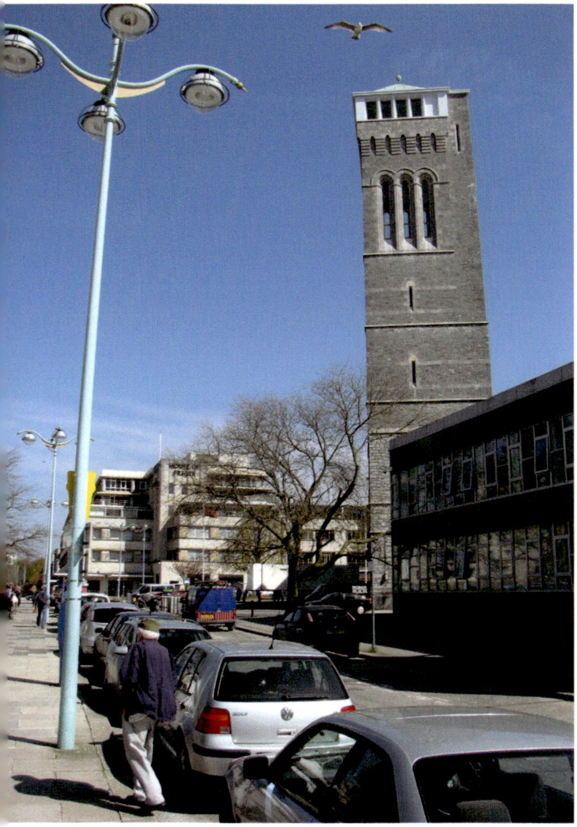

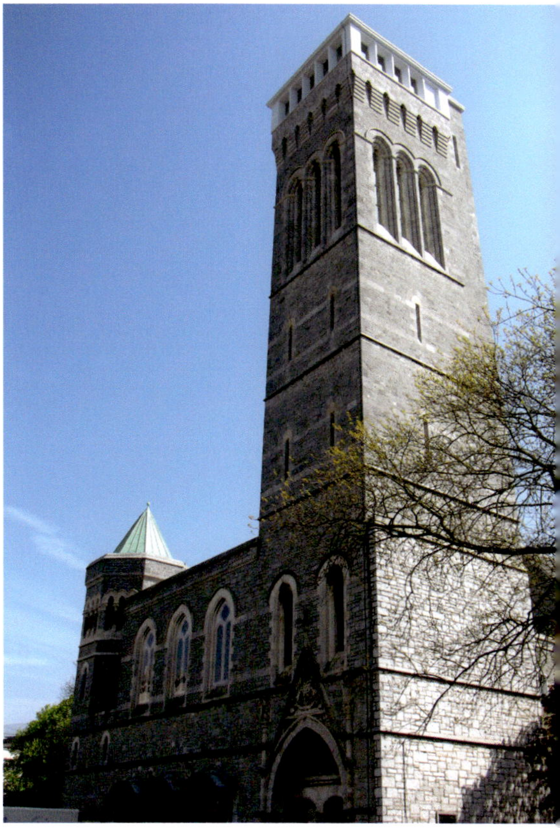

Above left: The tower of the Guildhall from Armada Way.

Above right: The imposing Guildhall building.

later. The Guildhall was reopened by Field Marshal the Viscount Montgomery of Alamein on 24 September 1959.

Fourteen stained-glass windows line the Great Hall and these were designed by Frederick Halford Coventry. They depict moments in Plymouth's history. At the front of the hall is a large tapestry which depicts Raphael's vision of the Miraculous Drought of Fishes. Status Quo appeared at the hall in 1973, followed by Queen the next year. The hall currently hosts graduations, award ceremonies, weddings and civil ceremonies, as well as collectors' markets.

The building is Grade II listed.

26. The Dingles Building

The E. Dingle & Co. building opened in Royal Parade in September 1951. The building was part of the regeneration of Plymouth and was the first new

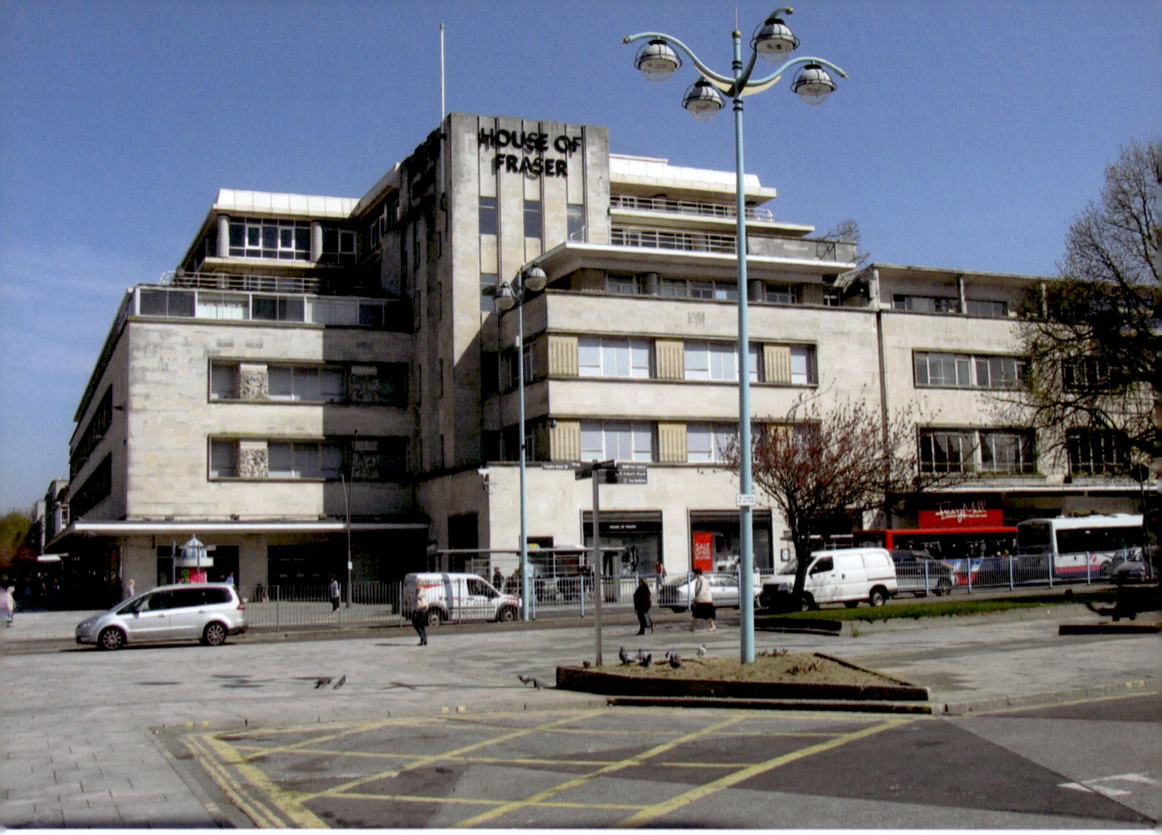

Above: The House of Fraser building on Royal Parade.

Below left: A close-up of the House of Fraser building from Plymouth Guildhall.

Below right: The House of Fraser building from Armada Way.

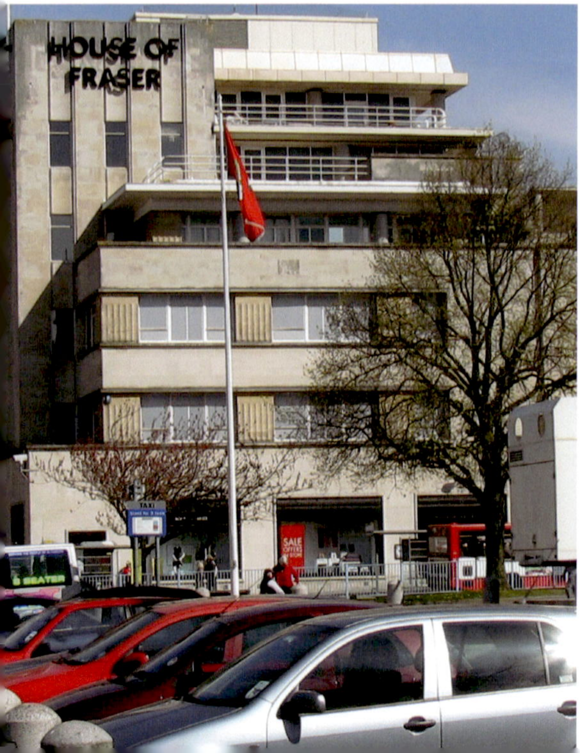

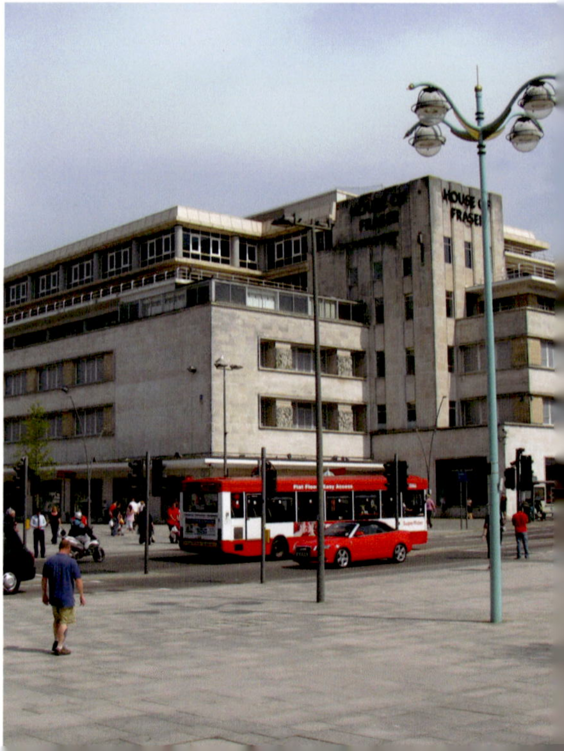

department store to open in the UK since 1938. Originally, the building had four floors together with 148,000 square feet of retail space. In later years, further floors were added including a restaurant on the top floor.

Previously, Edward Dingle had had a drapery shop at No. 30 Bedford Street, which opened in 1880. Within a year, the business grew and employed twenty-seven workers. By 1926, the business expanded, taking in Nos 28–31 Bedford Street and Nos 4–6 Cornwall Street.

In 1935, E. Dingle & Co. purchased their neighbour's business, a gents' outfitters, at Nos 26–27 Bedford Street. The gents' outfitters had traded as W. J. Vickery & Co. Ltd and the two owners, brothers Stanley and Ralph Vickery, joined the board of Dingles. The company further expanded and purchased the lease of No. 32 Bedford Street. They had eighty departments and employed over 500 staff.

On the night of 21 March 1941, heavy German bombing destroyed the nearby Yeo building and the fire destroyed the premises belonging to Dingles. They continued to trade, renting out vacant properties across the city.

When the war ended, Dingles were given a site near to their old premises as part of Patrick Abercrombie's reconstruction plan for Plymouth. The company was restructured in 1948 and work started on the new store the following year.

In 1954, Dingles was floated as a public company and expanded greatly in the 1960s, purchasing several department stores.

The House of Fraser bought out Dingles in 1971 but retained the company's name.

In December 1988, a fire devastated the top floor of the building in Royal Parade but this was rebuilt at a cost of £13,200,000. In the same year, the company changed their name from E. J. Dingle & Co. Ltd to House of Fraser (Twelve) Ltd, although stores continue to use the Dingles name.

In 2006, the Dingles name on the building was removed and replaced by the House of Fraser branding.

27. The Theatre Royal

The Theatre Royal was designed by the Peter Moro Partnership in 1977. They had a history of designing theatres around the UK. The builders were Messrs Richard Costain Ltd. Work on the building commenced in 1979 on land at the bottom of Royal Parade and took almost three years.

The theatre was officially opened by Princess Margaret on 5 May 1982. Also present at the opening was the Lord Mayor, Ralph Morrell. Following a fanfare from the band of Her Majesty's Royal Marines, the actor Leonard Rossiter made a speech on the opening day. Appearing in the opening show were Dickie Henderson, Iris Williams, the Melody Attlas Dancers, Keith Harris and Orville, Galina Samsova and David Ashmole from the Royal Ballet, Diane Montague from

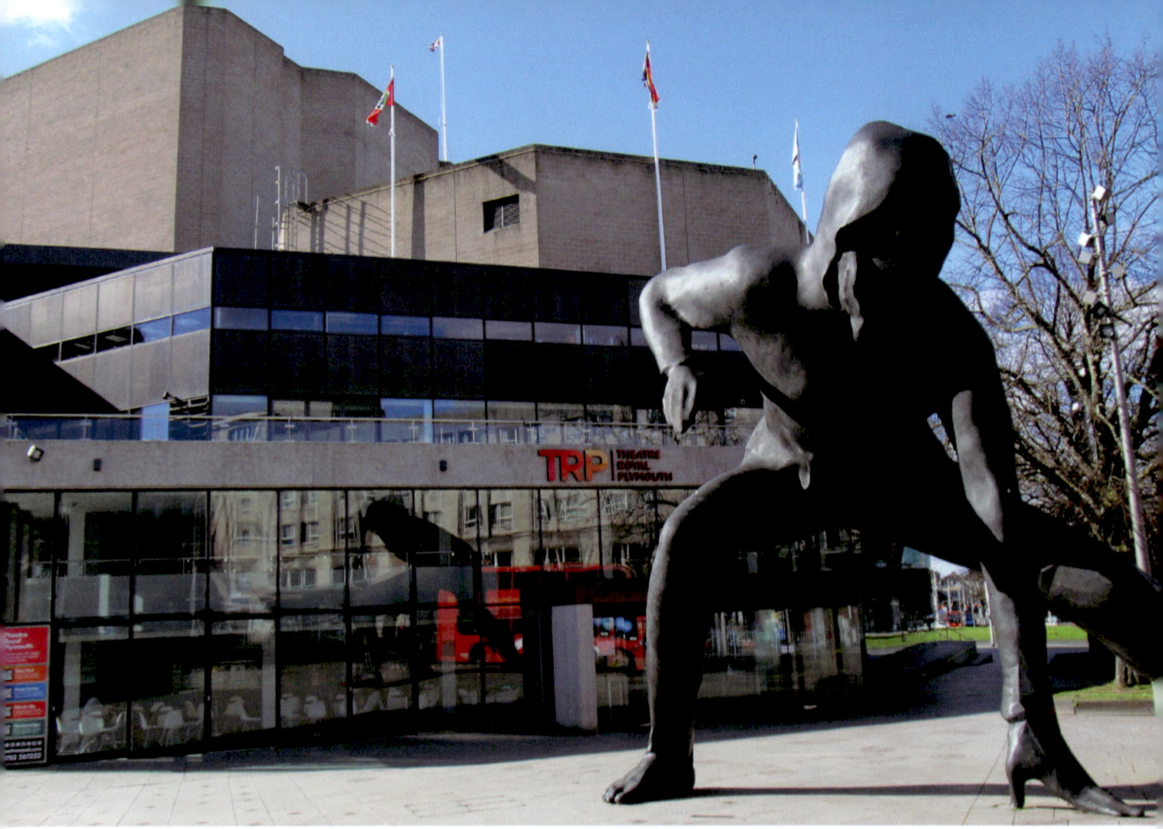

Above: The giant imposing *Messenger* statue in front of the Theatre Royal.

Below left: Derry's Clock with the Theatre Royal behind.

Below right: The front of the Theatre Royal. The statue of *Messenger* can be seen reflected in the window.

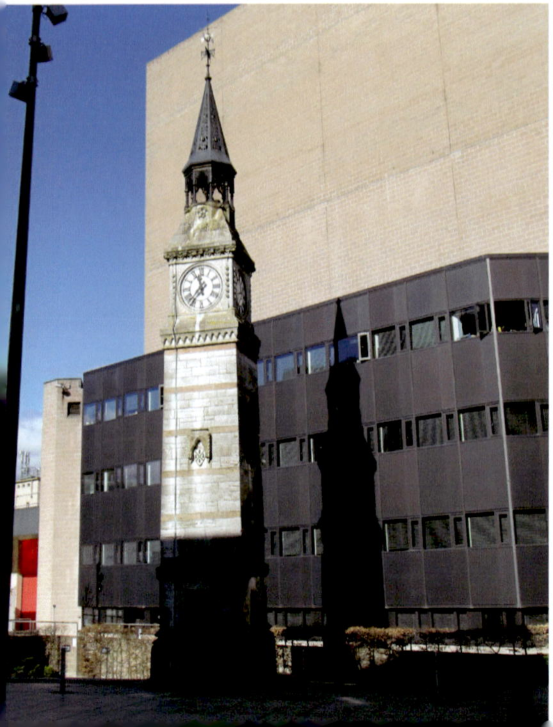

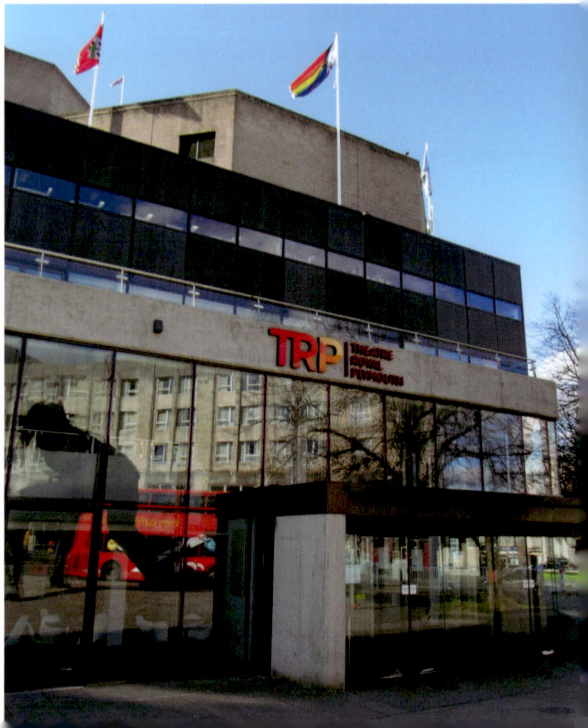

the Royal Opera House and the Massed Bands of Her Majesty's Royal Marines. Top of the bill was Gene Pitney.

The building consists of the Lyric, the theatre's main auditorium; the Drum, consisting of 200 seats; and the Lab, which has fifty seats. The Lyric hosts large-scale musicals and can seat 1,300 people.

In 2019, a 7-metre-high bronze sculpture called *Messenger* was unveiled outside the theatre. It was met with a mixed reaction: some people loved it while others found it overbearing and out of place. It was created by the Cornish artist Joseph Hillier and represents a female actor crouching and preparing to run onstage. The sculpture depicts a pose by cast member Nicola Kavanagh, during rehearsals for the Shakespeare play *Othello* in 2014. After *Messenger* was installed, the actress said of the sculpture, 'She's brave, she's not afraid. She is ready for anything that comes her way. If one little girl in Plymouth or anywhere else sees her and is inspired that would be great. There aren't that many statues of women and those that are around are passive, demure or looking beautiful. She looks like she's engaging and acting in a rebellious manner. I have two nieces, I think it's very important that little girls and little boys see women doing things – and you can't miss *Messenger*.'

28. The Western Morning News Building

Sir Harold Harmsworth opened the offices of the *Western Morning News* in Frankfort Street on 1 December 1938. Also at the opening ceremony were the Mayor and Mayoress of Plymouth, Mr and Mrs G. S. Scoble, as well as the Deputy Mayoress, Mrs H. G. Mason, and Mr James L. Palmer, the editor-in-chief, Mr J. Nott, the general manager and secretary, and Mr F. H. Padfield, the London manager.

The building was known as Leicester Harmsworth House and boasted that it was the most modern and well equipped newspaper office and printing works in the country.

The building was designed in Queen Anne style by the architects Herbert O. Ellis & Clarke. It was built by J. W. Spencer of St Lawrence Yard in Plymouth.

Due to a fear of future air raids, the floors and staircase of the building were constructed of solid concrete. The construction proved crucial to its survival during the bombing raids of 1941. The front of the ground floor was faced with Portland stone with 2-inch thick, handmade, sand-faced bricks above this.

Carved into the balconies was the West Country coat of arms, which was used over the leader in the *Western Morning News*. A large clock stood prominent on the front of the building. The floor of the building's entrance was paved with black and white tiles leading to a large pine staircase. On the first floor were the editorial offices while the second floor housed the managerial staff, a boardroom and the staff dining area. The third floor was used as a storeroom.

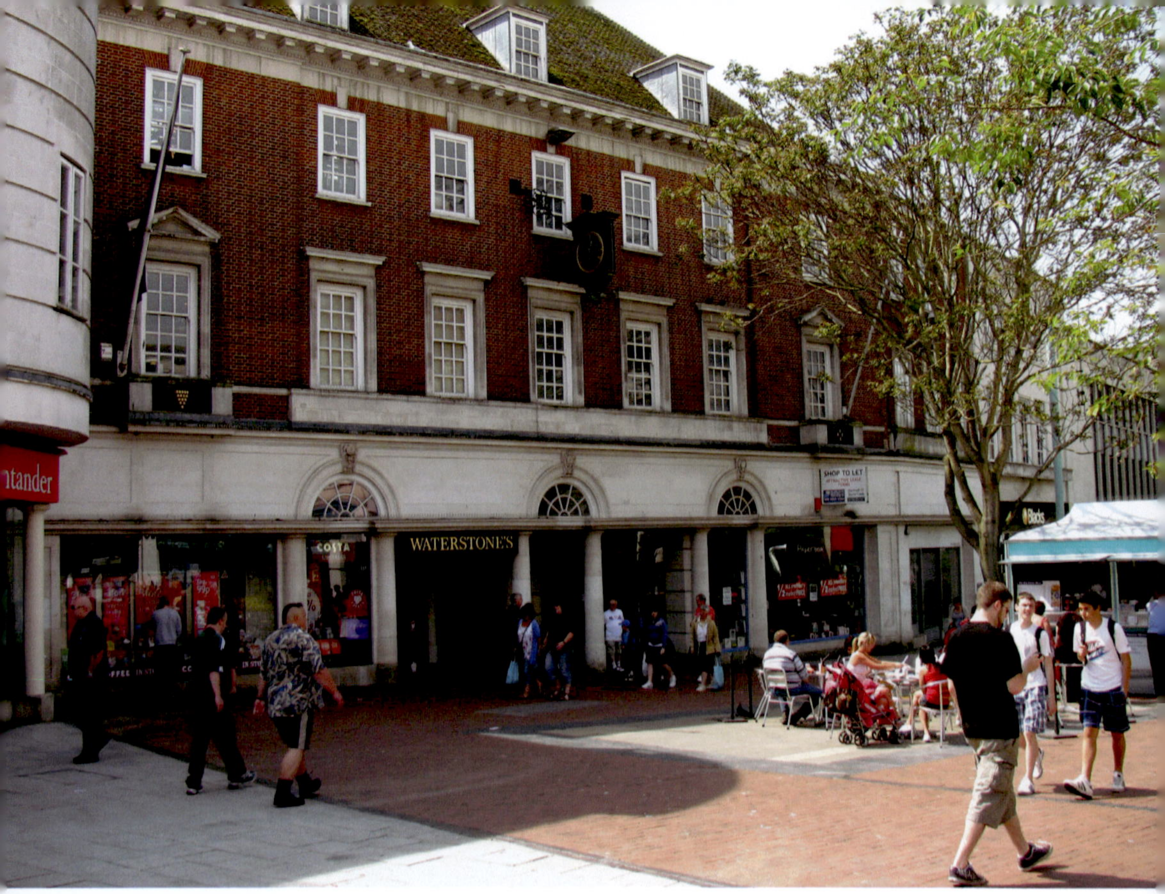

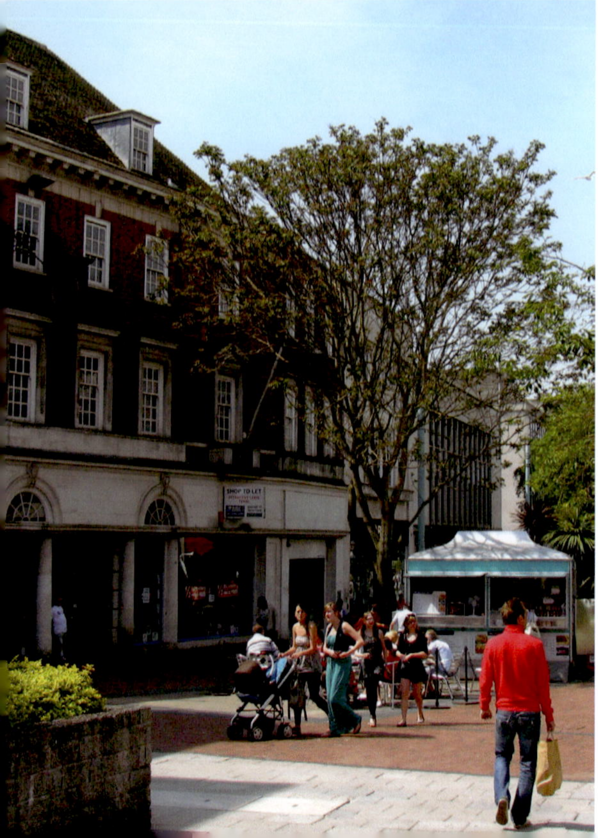

Above: The *Western Morning News* building in New George Street. Waterstones was still trading there when the photo was taken.

Left: A view of the *Western Morning News* building looking down New George Street.

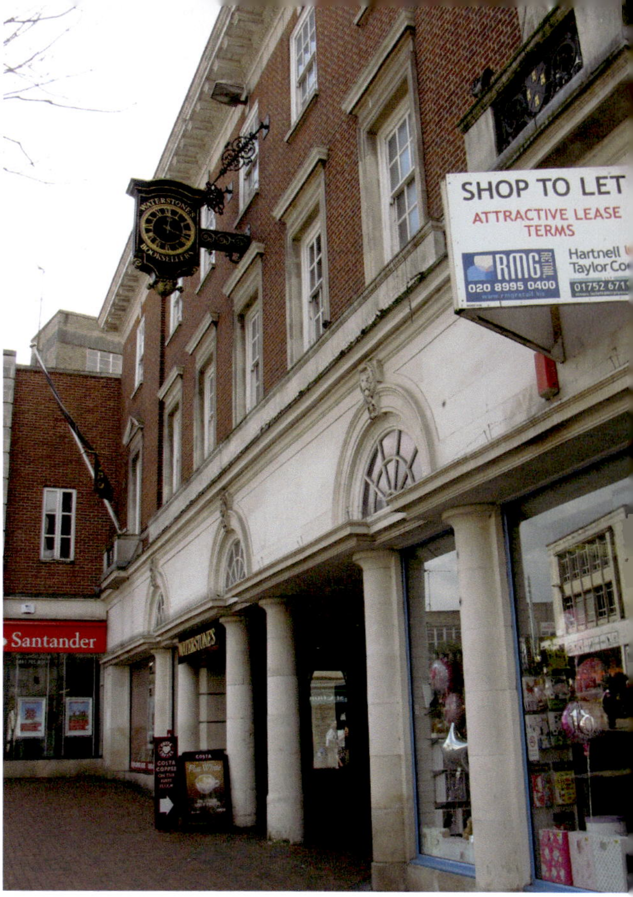

The entrance and the clock of the *Western Morning News* building.

Leicester Harmsworth House was one of the few buildings in the centre of Plymouth that survived the heavy bombing during the Second World War. The printing works to the rear and photographic records, however, were destroyed. The building continued as a newspaper office for many decades before being stripped and turned into retail premises, the most well-known being Waterstones, the bookshop (now gone). Once a classic building, it now looks worse for wear.

29. Plymouth Market

There has been a market in Plymouth since 1253. When the city was devastated by heavy bombing in 1941, many of the larger businesses moved into the previous Pannier Market. These included Marks and Spencers, Costers and Boots. The former Pannier Market was located south of what was Mill Street, which was located close to where the top of Cornwall Street now runs. The market was a central part of the community and many traders continued their businesses when their premises were destroyed by enemy bombing.

As part of the rebuilding of Plymouth, work started on the present market in 1952 and was completed in 1959. The building was designed by local architects

Walls and Pearn for Plymouth City Council. Sculptor David Weeks provided the wall art. The whole building was constructed from reinforced concrete.

The market hall measures 224 feet long and 148 feet wide, which is just over three quarters of an acre of floor space. The north lit shell-shaped concrete roof stands 57 feet above the market floor. The height of the structure and the expanse of glass make the market hall well lit, as well as being well ventilated and cool in summer.

Two businesses have remained in the market since it first opened in the late 1950s: Book Stall and Coronet Engravers.

During 2017, the market underwent a £3.5 million revamp, which included works to the concrete roof, the installation of solar panels and a new lift, together with improved ventilation and facilities for the many restaurants and businesses. The market held a Grand Day Out event in September 2017 to celebrate the reopening of the market after completion of its regeneration.

As with all the shops in the city, the market isn't as busy as it once was but is still an interesting place to visit with a vast array of goods available. Today's market is home to 140 stalls, eateries and cafés. The building is Grade II listed.

Shoppers inside the Pannier Market.

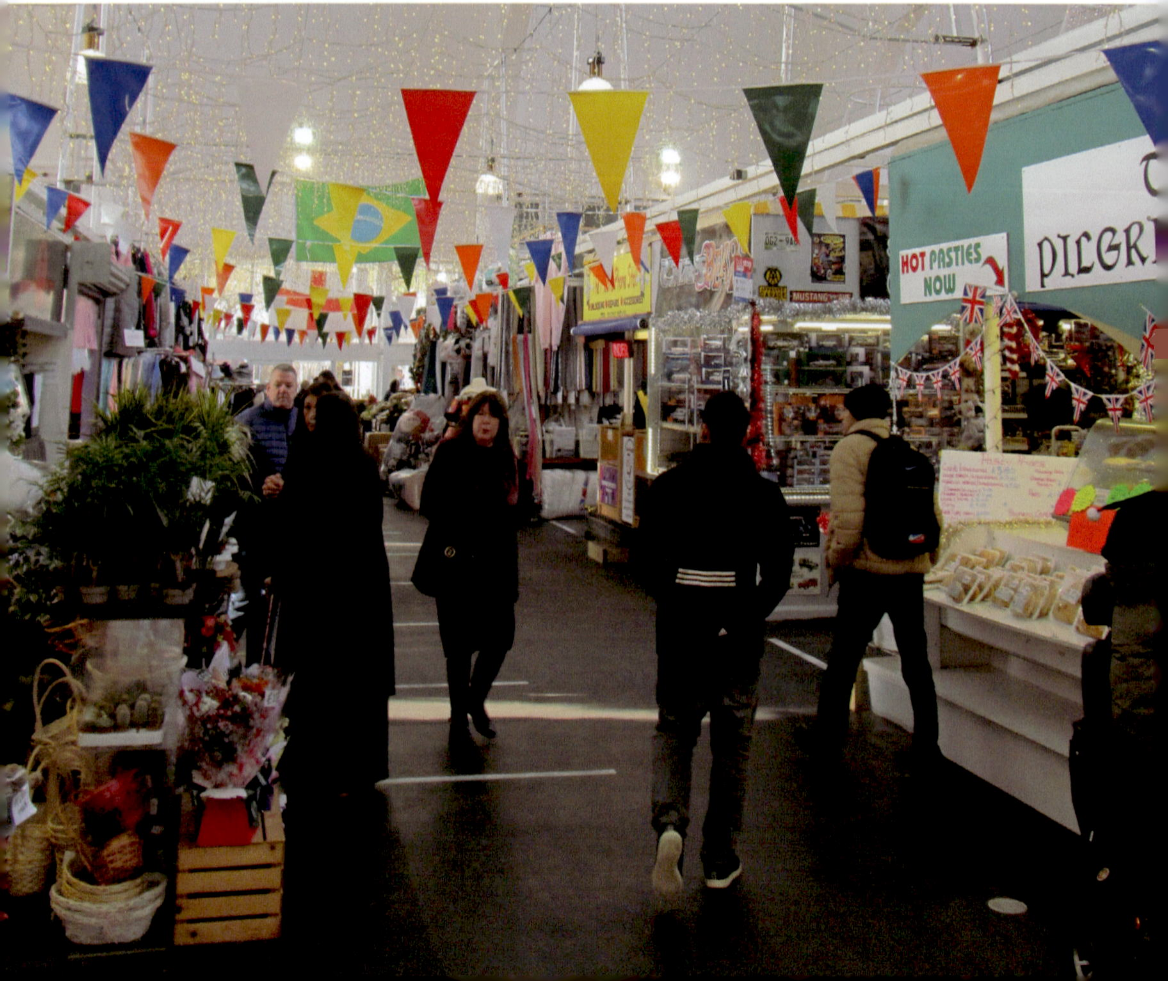

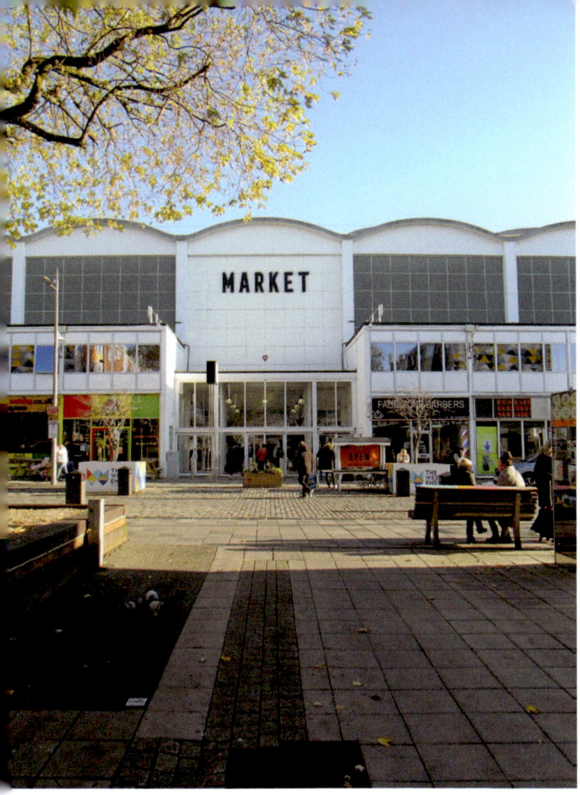

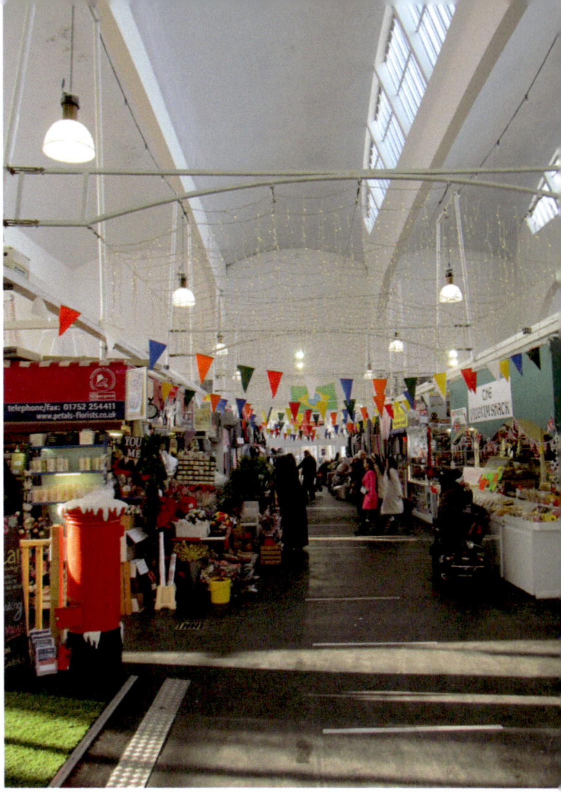

Above left: The entrance to the market from Frankfort Gate.

Above right: The airy and spacious interior of the Pannier Market.

30. The Bank

The building situated in Bank of England Place, George Street, was originally the Wiltshire and Dorset Bank and later became Lloyds. The Wiltshire and Dorset Bank was founded in 1835, although it didn't open its first branch in Plymouth until 1885. They were originally based at No. 57 George Street but purchased Harvey's Hotel in Lockyer Street in 1888 and had it converted and added to, making new bank chambers.

The architect of the new building was G. M. Silley, of No. 17 Craven Street, The Strand, London. The new building was completed in 1889 and built in the Italianate style.

The bank was built on a granite base with an ornamented frontage made of Bath stone with Portland stone capitals. The design continued to the first floor, with the second floor being square in shape and set back from the curved line. The height of the front of the building was 55 feet 6 inches.

Much of the former Harvey's Family Hotel became office and residential space. The hotel had formerly been known as George House and was the home to Sir George Magrath, a physician who served under Admiral Lord Nelson. When Magrath died in 1857, the property remained empty until 1862 before opening as Harvey's Family Hotel. The new hotel was described as being 'replete with

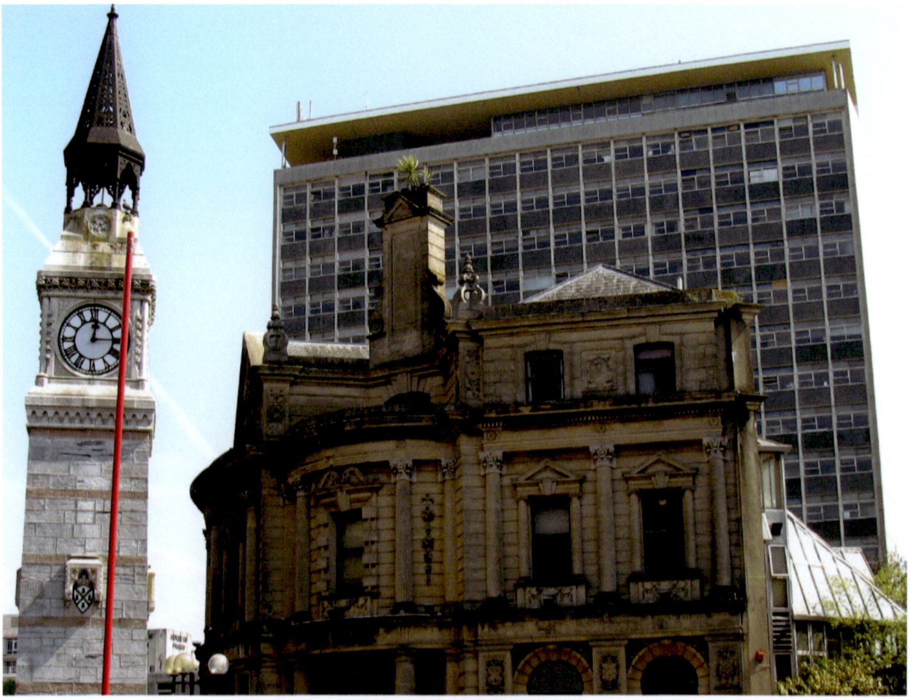

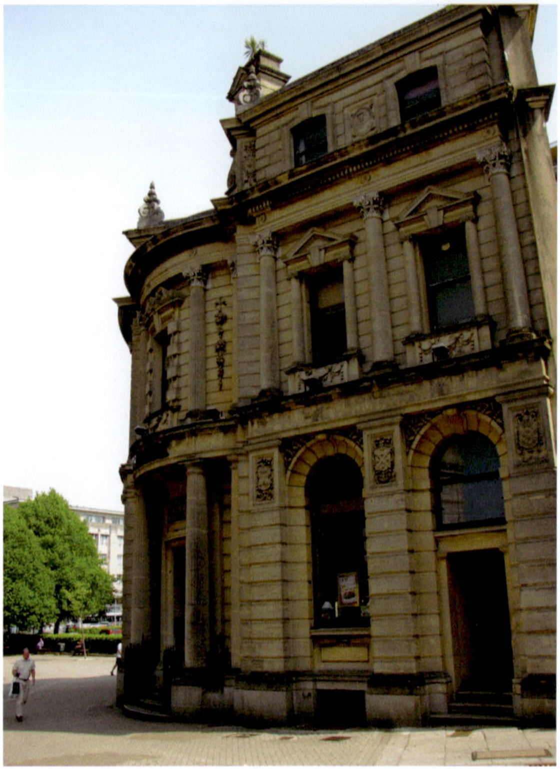

Above: The Bank public house with Derry's Clock in the foreground and the Civic Centre in the background.

Left: A view of the Bank looking towards Royal Parade.

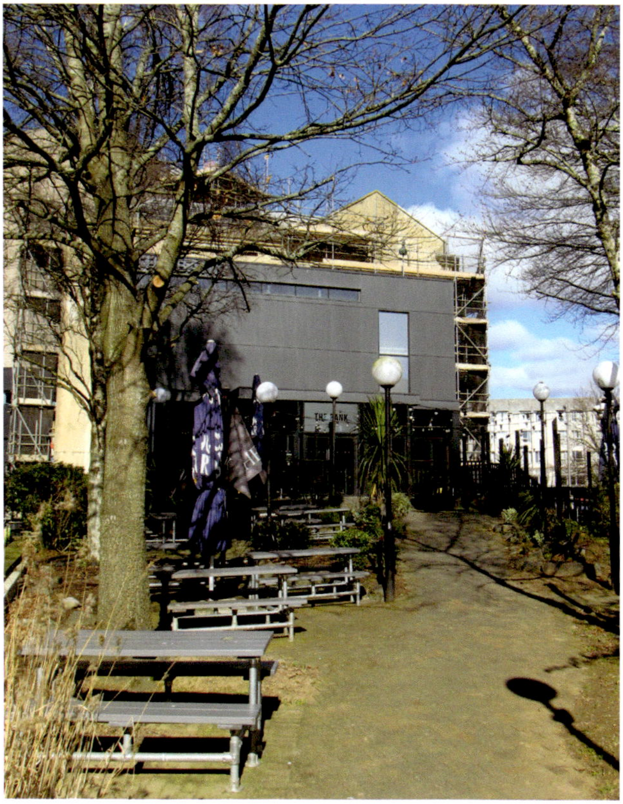

The rear beer garden of the Bank public house.

every comfort, convenience and accommodation for families visiting the locality – including hot and cold baths'.

The area was devastated in the Second World War but the bank and Derry's Clock survived together with the building. This later became the Lockyer Hotel and then the Lockyer Tavern before being demolished in the early 1980s. The wall around the garden area of the Bank public house is all that remains of the Lockyer Tavern.

The Bank building was Grade II listed in 1975 and turned into a public house in 1982. In 1986, a conservatory area was added to the building but this was removed in 2019 and replaced by an orangery.

31. St Andrew's Church

St Andrew's Church is located on the southern side of Royal Parade. A church is believed to have stood there since before 1264, possibly dating back to Saxon times. The tower dates from 1461 and the labour to build it was paid for by a wealthy local merchant, Thomas Yogge. The tower stands 136 feet and 6 inches tall.

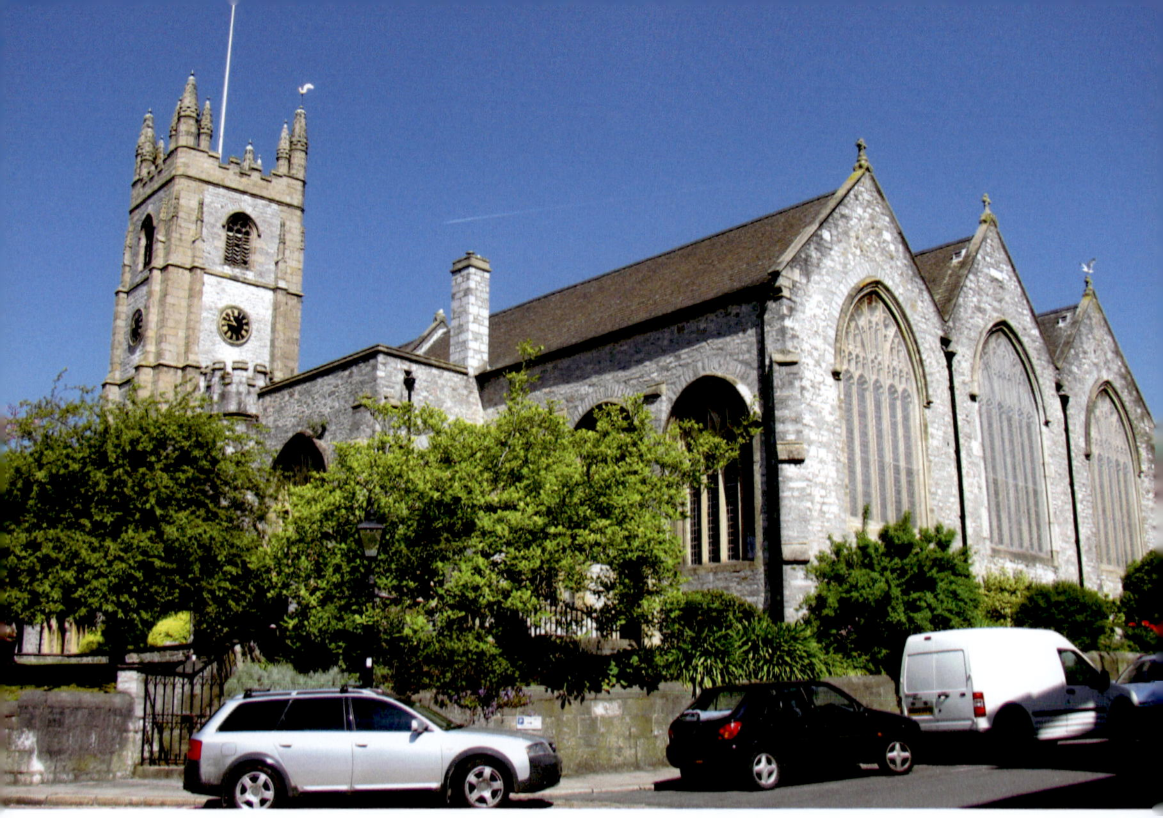

Above: St Andrew's Church from Finewell Street.

Below left: Inside St Andrew's Church showing its magnificent stained-glass windows.

Below right: The clock tower of St Andrew's Church.

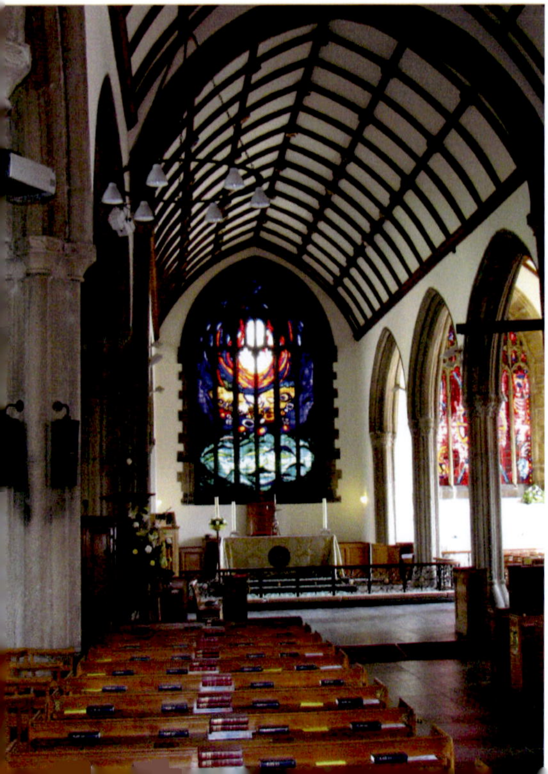

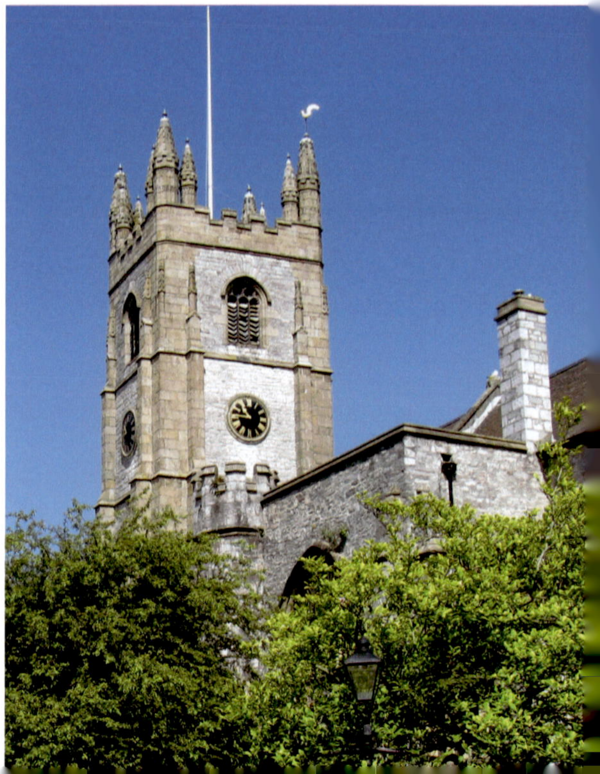

It was known as the mother church of Plymouth and William de la Stane was the first recorded vicar there in 1264. It is the largest parish church in Devon, measuring 184 feet long and 69 feet wide.

Catherine of Aragon attended the church in 1501 to give thanks for a safe passage from Spain. Francis Drake, John Hawkins and Charles II also visited St Andrew's. Admiral Blake's heart is buried in the church. On 15 August 1657, he died aboard his flagship the *St George* after defeating the Spanish West Indian fleet at the Battle of Santa Cruz de Tenerife. His death occurred as the ship entered Plymouth Sound. Originally, he was given a state burial at St Margaret's Church in Westminster, which was attended by Oliver Cromwell, but upon the restoration of the monarchy, his body was exhumed in 1661 on the orders of King Charles II and deposited in a common grave together with the remains of Cromwell. William Bligh was baptised at St Andrew's in 1754. The church was restored by John Foulston in 1824 and later by Sir George Gilbert Scott in 1875.

During the blitz, the church was badly damaged leaving only the walls and tower remaining. The morning after St Andrew's Church was bombed, a headmistress placed a wooden sign over the north door with the word '*Resurgam*' written on it, meaning, in Latin, 'I will rise again'. An open-air service was held, weather permitting, every Sunday at 8 p.m. during the summer months.

Frederick Etchells restored and re-roofed the church and it was reconsecrated on St Andrew's Day on 30 November 1957. The restoration included a new chancel. The word '*Resurgam*' is now carved in stone above the main door.

32. The National Provincial Bank

The National Provincial Bank stands at the top of Royal Parade. Work started on the building in 1956 as part of the reconstruction of Plymouth. The bank was built by Messrs Humphreys Ltd, of London, Chester and Plymouth, and the granite portico, facings and paving were sourced from the Dartmoor Granite Company located at Merrivale Quarries close to Princetown. The clock tower, counters and bank fittings were furnished by Maple-Martyn of London and Cheltenham. After the war, Maple-Martyn had been engaged in the manufacturing of internal woodwork for prefabricated houses. They later returned to furnishing cruise ships.

The National Provincial Bank building was completed in 1958 and opened to the public on Monday 15 September at 9.30 a.m. of that year. The bank manager was Mr G. A. Blakey.

Before the Blitz of Plymouth, the National Provincial Bank had been located at No. 35 Bedford Street. It opened its first branch in Devonport in 1839 after acquiring the Devonport General Bank. In 1878, the bank opened a permanent branch in Plymouth, which was located at Westwell Street before moving to premises at No. 68 George Street in 1884.

On 16 April 1903, the National Provincial Bank moved into the ground floor of the recently built Prudential Building situated at the junction of Bedford Street, Frankfort Street and George Street. The bank moved to No. 35 Bedford Street in 1927 after the premises were extended and remained there during the air raids of 1941, which caused extensive damage to the building. However, the bank still managed to trade from the ground floor and remained at Bedford Street until May 1949. After that, they moved to the former Bank of England premises in Bank of England Place. The manager of the bank, Mr H. E. Mitchell, was also the manager

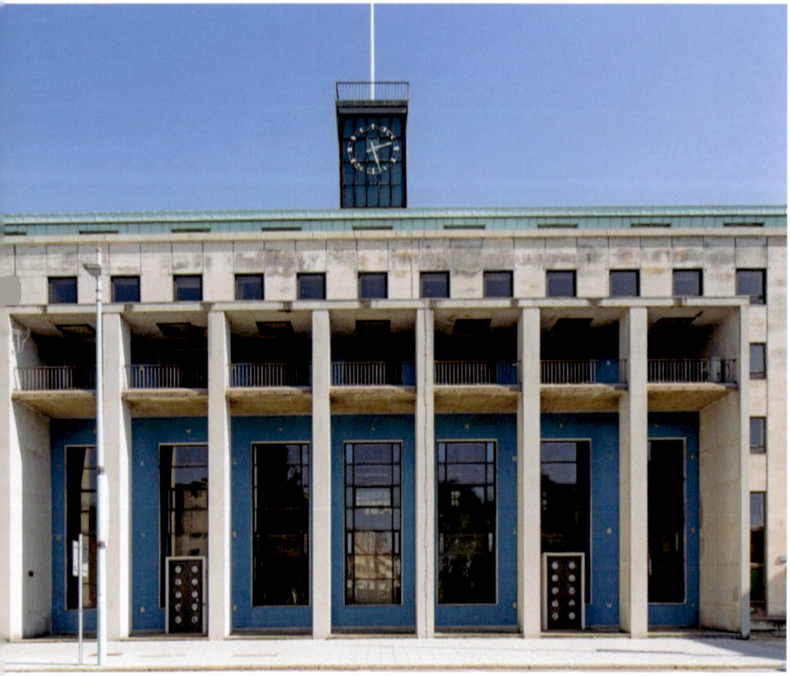

The front of the old National Provincial Bank.

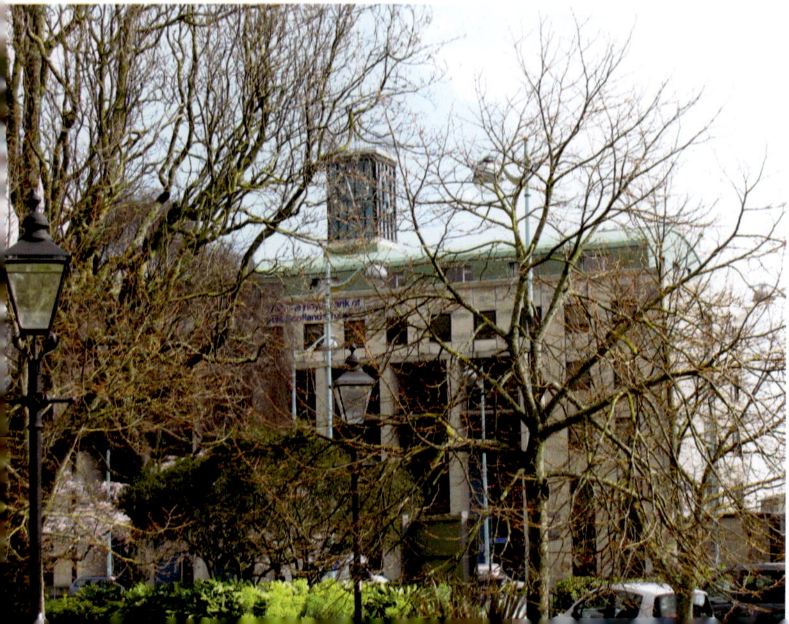

Looking towards the National Provincial Bank from St Andrew's Church.

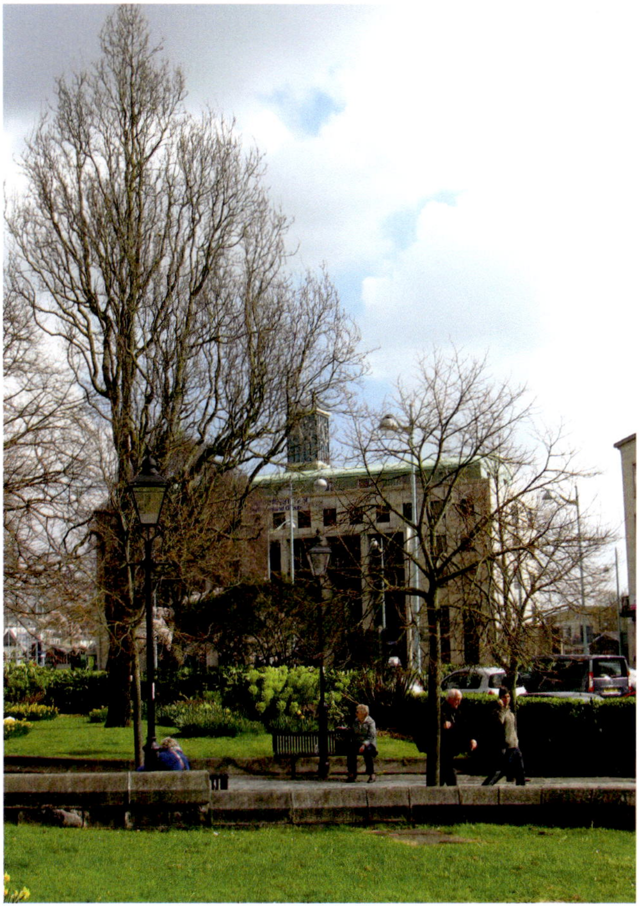

The tree-lined area in front of St Andrew's Church looking towards the National Provincial Bank.

of their branch at No. 63 Mutley Plain. Several years after, they moved into the iconic building at St Andrew's Cross on Royal Parade.

Today, the building houses the Royal Bank of Scotland.

33. Charles Church

Work on Charles Church began in 1641 after Charles I gave his permission for Plymouth to build another church. The land where the church stands was given by William Warren, a wine merchant, in return for receiving a burial plot adjoining the chancel and a seat from which to 'hear divine service and the word of God preached'. By 1643, the building had reached roof level and the first baptism took place later that year. Work on the church was interrupted by the English Civil War between 1642 and 1652 but the main part of the building was completed by 1658. In September 1665, the church was consecrated by the Bishop of Exeter, Seth Ward.

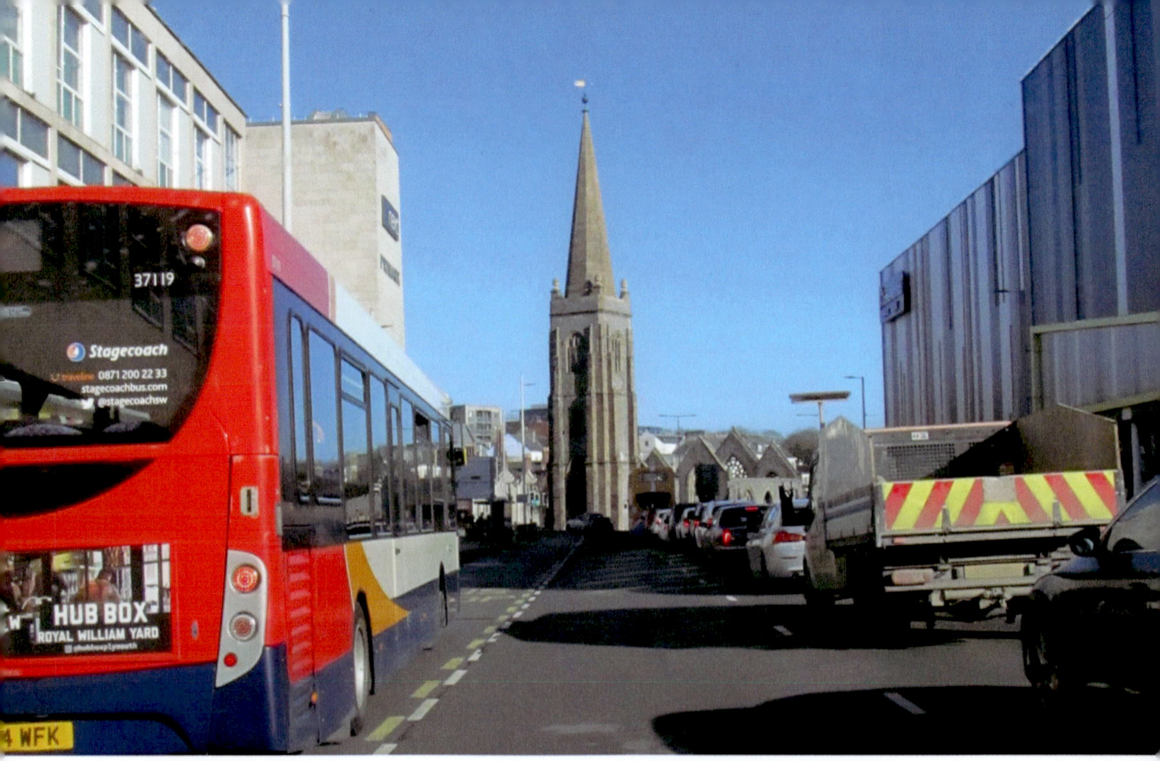

Above: Approaching the ruins of Charles Church from Old Town Street.

Below left: Charles Church sitting in the middle of the roundabout at Charles Cross.

Below right: A plaque on the wall within Charles Church.

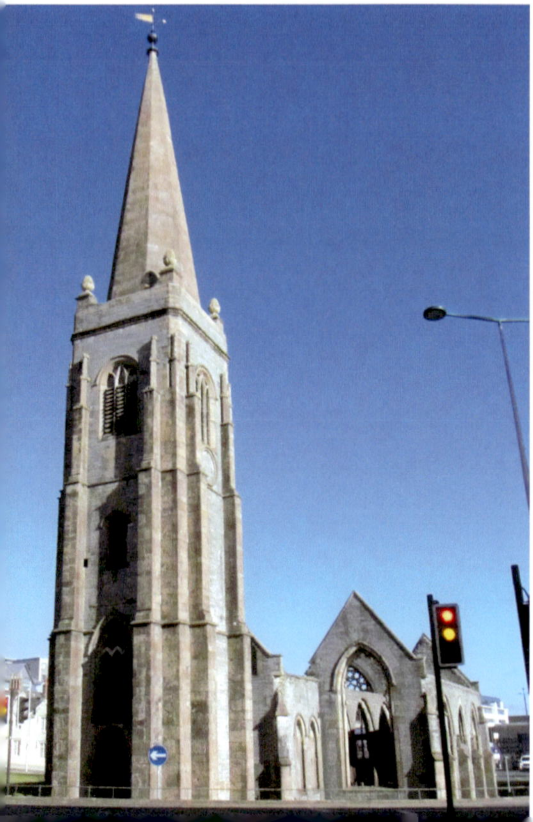

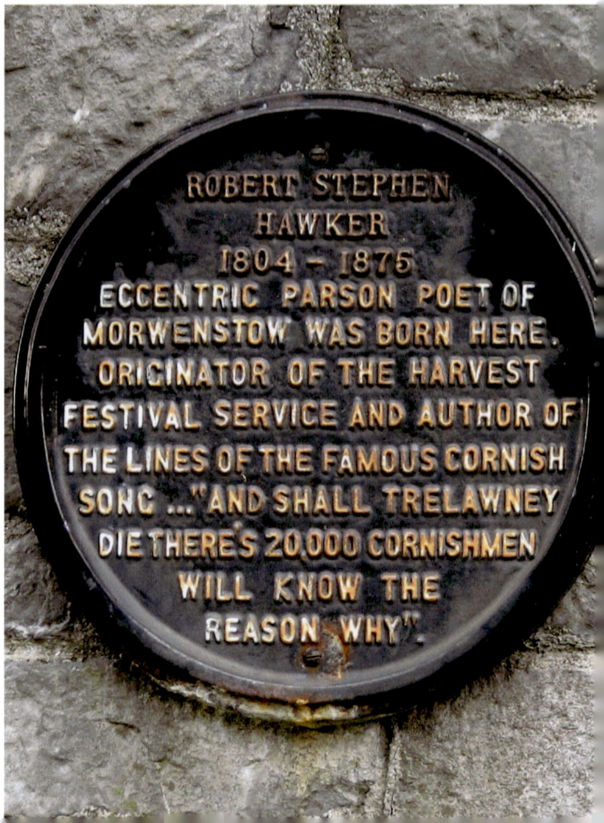

The church had a wooden spire covered in lead, which was added in 1708.This was replaced with a stone one in 1766. The church eventually contained ten bells. Joseph Jury supplied the first bells, which were cast in 1709. Jury also donated the clock and chimes in 1719. The clock had two faces, one on the north side and one on the south. In 1782, the bells were recast, with two more being added in 1856. The final bell was added in 1898.

Before the Second World War, the church stood in Vennel Street and was surrounded by a graveyard. It was destroyed by the heavy bombing during the Blitz of 1941. The bodies from the graveyard were reinterred at Efford Cemetery. The church was partially restored in 1957 and left as a monument to the civilians killed within the city during the Second World War. The city engineer, James Paton Watson, was the first person to suggest that the church should remain as a memorial to Plymouth's war dead when he prepared the Plan for Plymouth in 1943. However, the council's reconstruction committee decided in June 1953 that the church should be demolished. The decision was later made to save it.

Today, it stands in the middle of Charles Cross roundabout and is dwarfed by the Drake Circus Shopping Mall nearby. For many years, a multistorey car park stood where the Mall stands today.

34. The Drake Circus Shopping Centre

Drake Circus has seen many changes over the years. The area was once famous for its old buildings and the Guinness Clock, which many residents relied on to tell the time. Prior to the clock, there stood in its place a large illuminated sign advertising Bovril. The area that originally formed Drake Circus fell between Old Town Street, Ebrington Street and the junction of Tavistock Road and Park Street and included just six shops.

Demolition of the northern park of Drake Circus began in 1964 and three years later the lower part was demolished. A new two-storey development was began in 1968 and the new shopping centre was officially opened by Princess Anne in 1971. The shopping centre is well remembered for including C&A, Tesco and Arcadia, as well as smaller shops such as Purple Haze and the Christian bookshop.

In 2004, the area was redeveloped again and the new Drake Circus Shopping Mall was built to mixed reactions. Its bright, panelled frontage is easily recognisable and is in stark contrast to the ruin of Charles Church, which stands directly in front of it when travelling to the centre along Exeter Street. The latest incarnation opened in October 2006 and changed the top end of the city completely. The building was designed by London-based architects Chapman Taylor and was constructed by Bovis Lend Lease. The shopping centre was awarded the inaugural Carbuncle Cup for 'crimes against architecture' and was described as the worst new building in the UK. While many would have agreed with the award at the

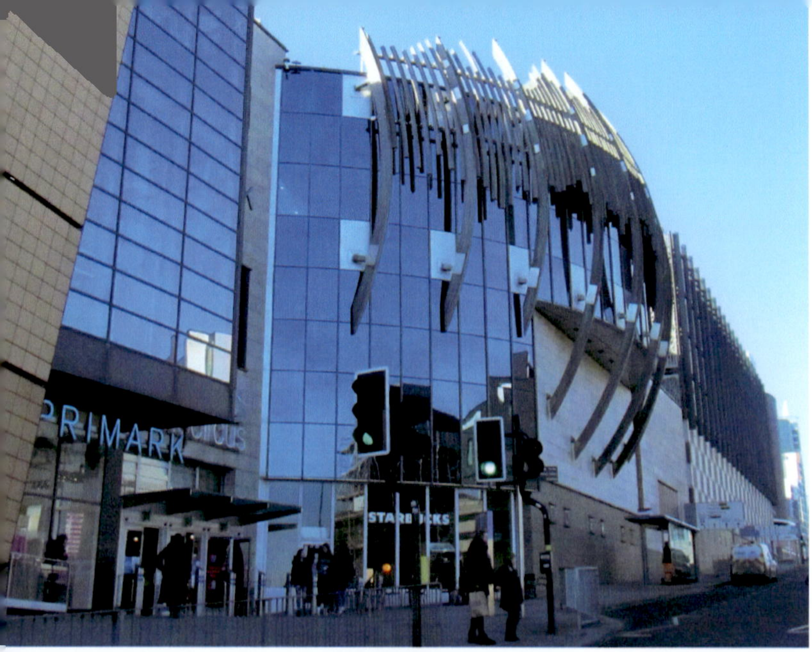

The reflective frontage of the Drake Circus Shopping Centre.

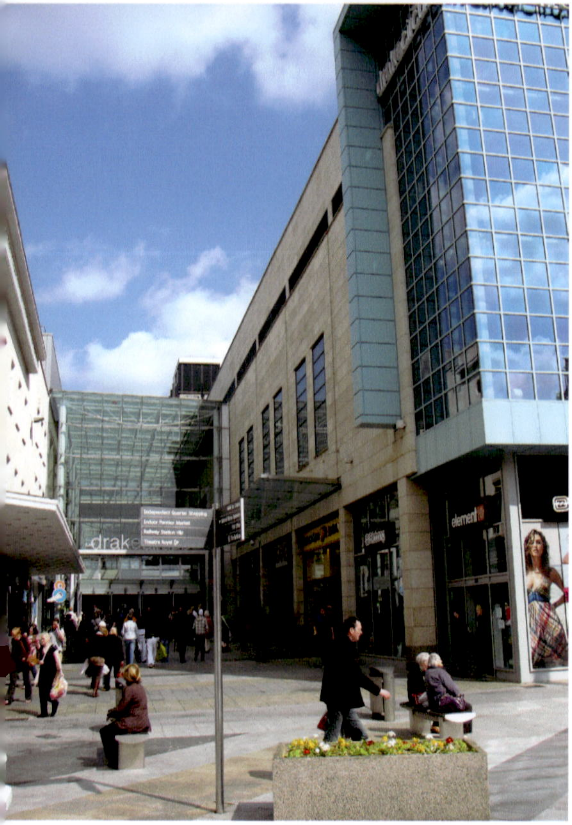

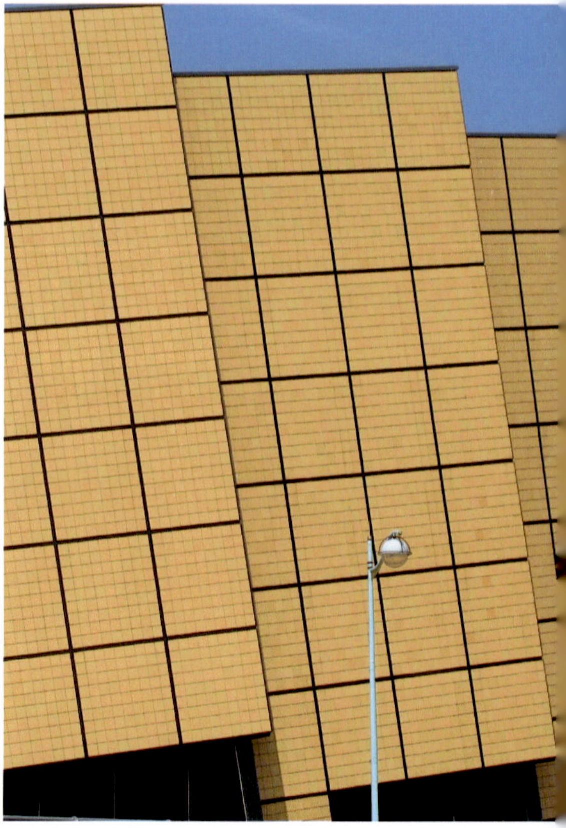

Above left: The entrance to Drake Circus Shopping Centre in New George Street.

Above right: The brightly coloured tiles adorning the Drake Circus Shopping Centre.

time, its strange appearance has grown on people over the years. In 2007, the shopping centre won two retail industry national awards including the *Retail Week* magazine's 'Shopping Location of the Year'.

The building has a retail floor space of 425,000 square feet and has more than sixty stores and restaurants. Shops contained within include Waterstones, Boots, Next and Primark.

35. The Box

Plymouth's first museum was in the Athenaeum building in George Street adjacent to the Theatre Royal. In 1898, a museum was opened in Beaumont House eventually followed by the main museum in Tavistock Road.

In 1906, Doctor Andrew Carnegie donated £15,000 towards the building of a new public library. It was decided that a museum should be built alongside the library in Tavistock Road at a cost of £13,000. The building was designed by Thornely and Rooke of Plymouth and built by Pethick Brothers Limited, who commenced work on 9 December 1907. The library cost £15,627 to build while the museum cost £13,313.

On 16 October 1907, the foundation stone for the Plymouth Museum and Art Gallery in Tavistock Road was laid. The museum opened to the public in 1910. On show was an Egyptian display, stuffed animal and bird exhibits, and an art gallery, as well as statues and artifacts from around the world. A pair of Robert Falcon Scott's skis were put on display near to the entrance. Although they originally were the property of Scott, they were later used by fellow Terra Nova Expedition member Patrick Keohane and he gifted them to the city. They proved to be a very popular exhibit.

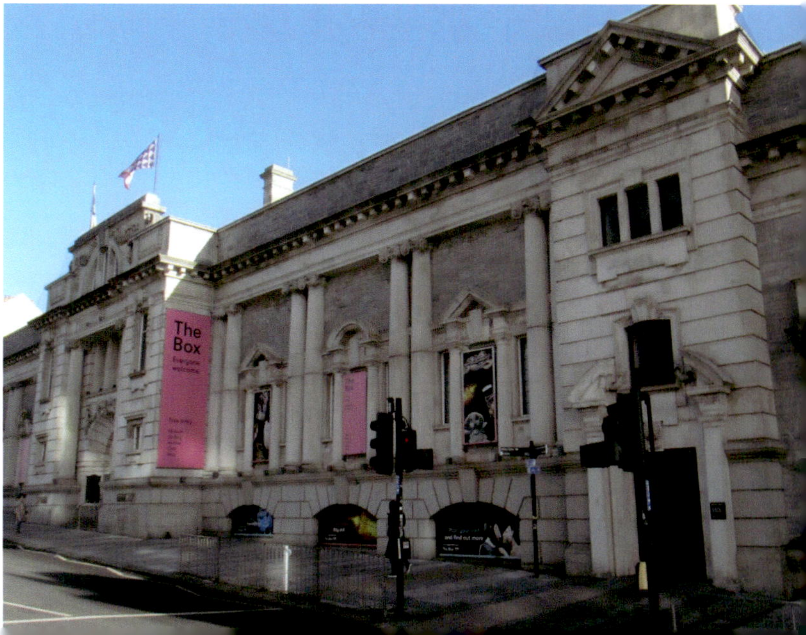

The front of the old museum and library, now The Box.

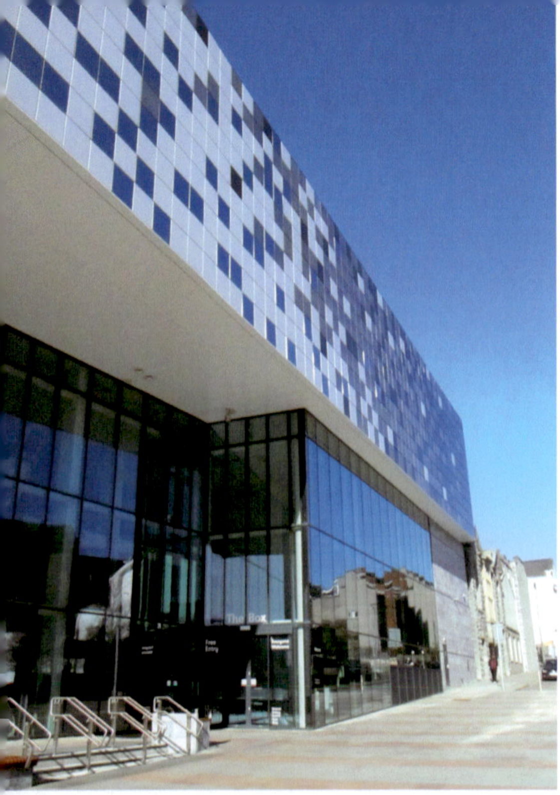

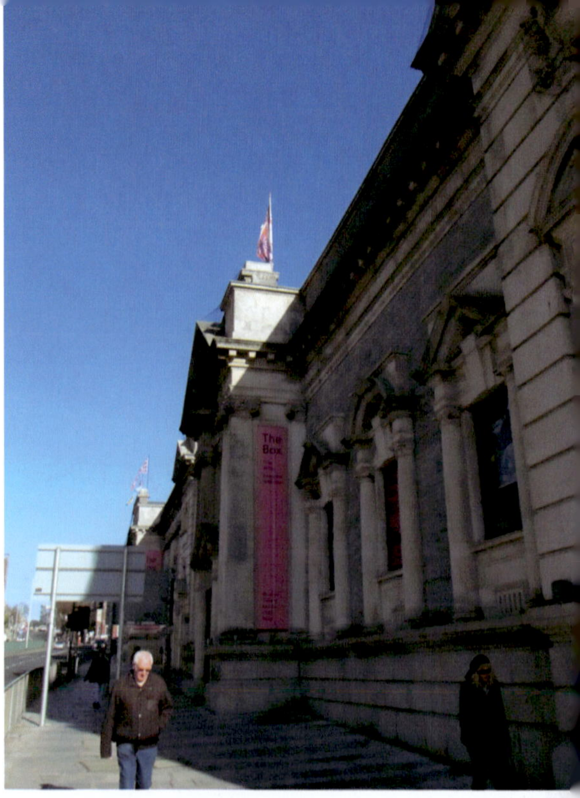

Above left: The rear modern entrance to The Box in Tavistock Place.

Above right: The ornate frontage of The Box looking towards North Hill.

The building remained untouched for over 100 years until it was decided that the city needed a new, more modern, museum. Work commenced on the building of The Box in January 2017 and combined the library and museum building. It opened in October 2020 and houses the museum, art gallery and local studies library, as well as the Plymouth and West Devon Record Office, the South West Image Bank and the South West Film and Television Archive. A popular attraction is a full-size mammoth, known as Mildred, which was manufactured in Minnesota, USA. Another item relating to Robert Falcon Scott featured at The Box is his christening cup, dating from 1868, which was sold by Scott's son in the 1980s and purchased by Plymouth City Council Arts & Heritage.

36. The Beckley Point Building

For almost sixty years the YMCA building stood at the top of Cobourg Street before being replaced with Plymouth's tallest structure – Beckley Point. The YMCA building opened in 1958 and had 102 bedrooms and a restaurant. The upper floors were let to the Legal and General Insurance Company.

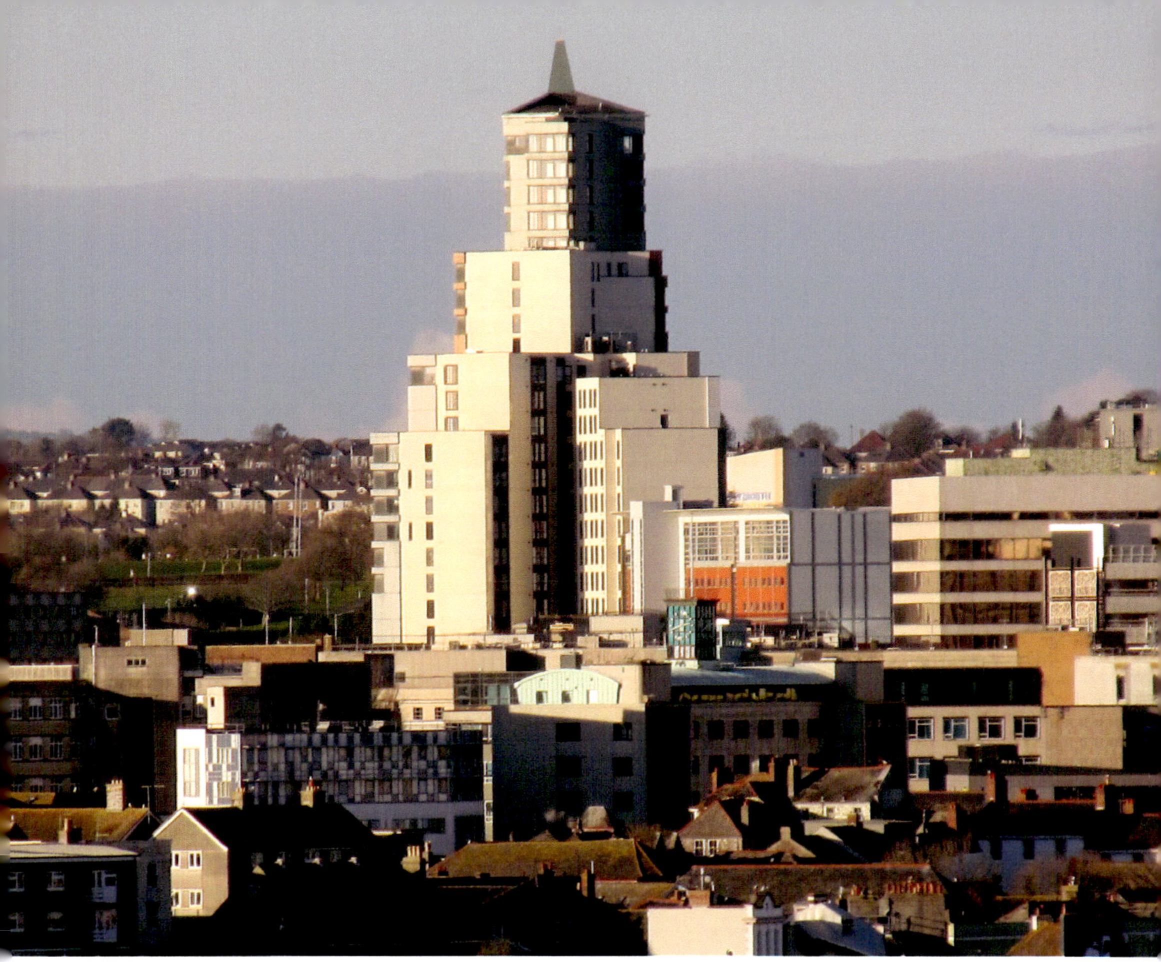

Above: The imposing Beckley Point building.

Right: Beckley Point from the railway station.

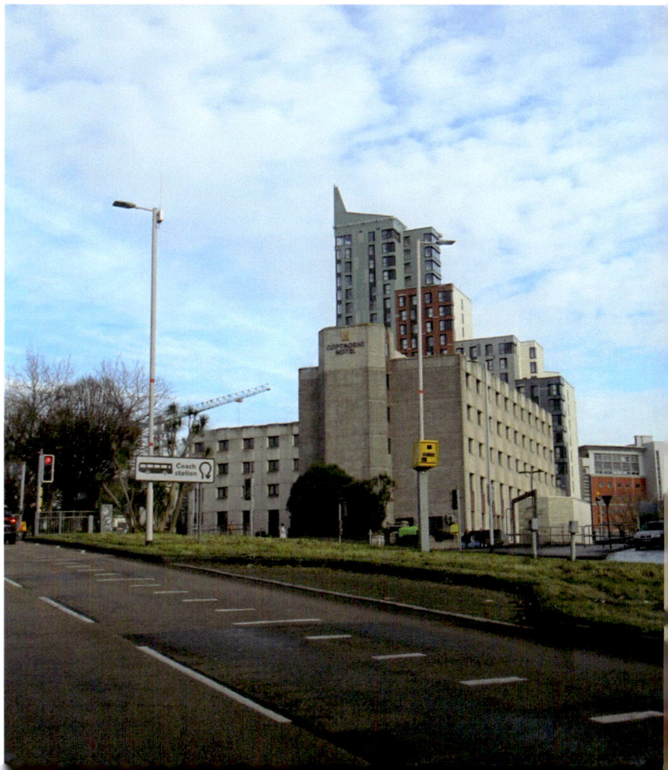

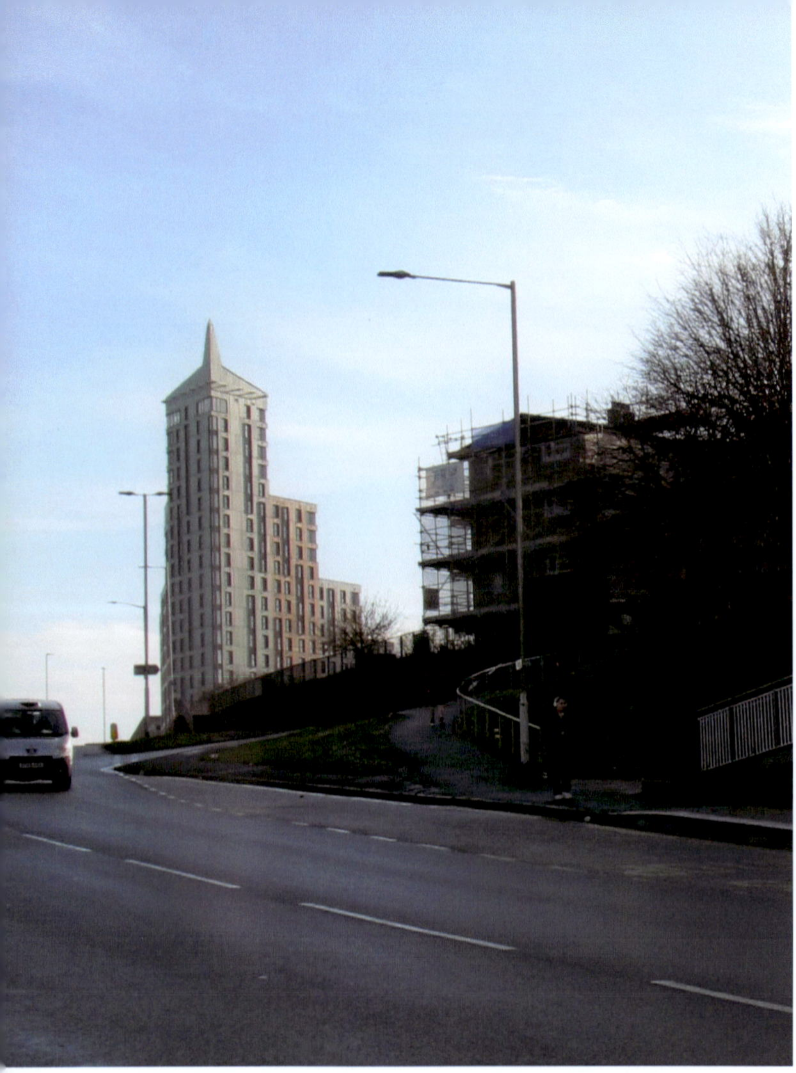

Looking ahead to Beckley Point from the road leading towards Western Approach.

Its replacement, Beckley Point, has twenty floors and stands 78 metres tall, making it twice the height of the Civic Centre. Boyes Rees Architects, based in London and Cardiff, designed the structure and the building work was carried out by contractors Kier. Beckley Point cost £30.79 million to build and houses 505 student flats. It was due to open in September 2017 but completion was delayed due to the devastating Grenfell Tower fire in London in June 2017. Cladding was deemed satisfactory on the Beckley Point Building but the decision was made to replace it as a precaution. The building still opened in September that year but the scaffold remained while the work was carried out.

Beckley Point includes six social spaces including a gaming room with eight screens, controllers and gaming chairs. There's also a dinner party kitchen, a study room, a cinema room, a common room with a pool table, TV, and a sky lounge taking in views across Plymouth. The building looks dynamic and very modern and can be seen from all over Plymouth, from the Hoe to Jennycliffe, as well as on the roads that approach the city.

As with the Drake Circus Shopping Centre, Beckley Point was nominated for the Carbuncle Cup, which is awarded by the architecture magazine *Building Design*. Its readers vote for which building they like the least in the previous twelve months. Although Beckley Point made it to a shortlist of six, the Carbuncle Cup ended up being awarded to the Redrock building in Stockport, Manchester.

37. Plymouth Railway Station, North Road

North Road station first opened in 1877 and was expanded in 1908. It was originally a joint station for the Great Western Railway and the London & South Western Railway. Colonel Yolland, the Board of Trade's Inspector, visited the station in February 1877 but was not satisfied enough to allow it to be opened to the public. The roof was incomplete and the Up platform still needed to be paved. Matters were sorted and North Road station opened to public traffic on Wednesday 28 March 1877.

The station was originally built of wood with the platforms fully covered by train sheds. There were originally two through platforms but further platforms were added when the station was expanded in 1908.

The glass frontage of the former Intercity House at North Road railway station.

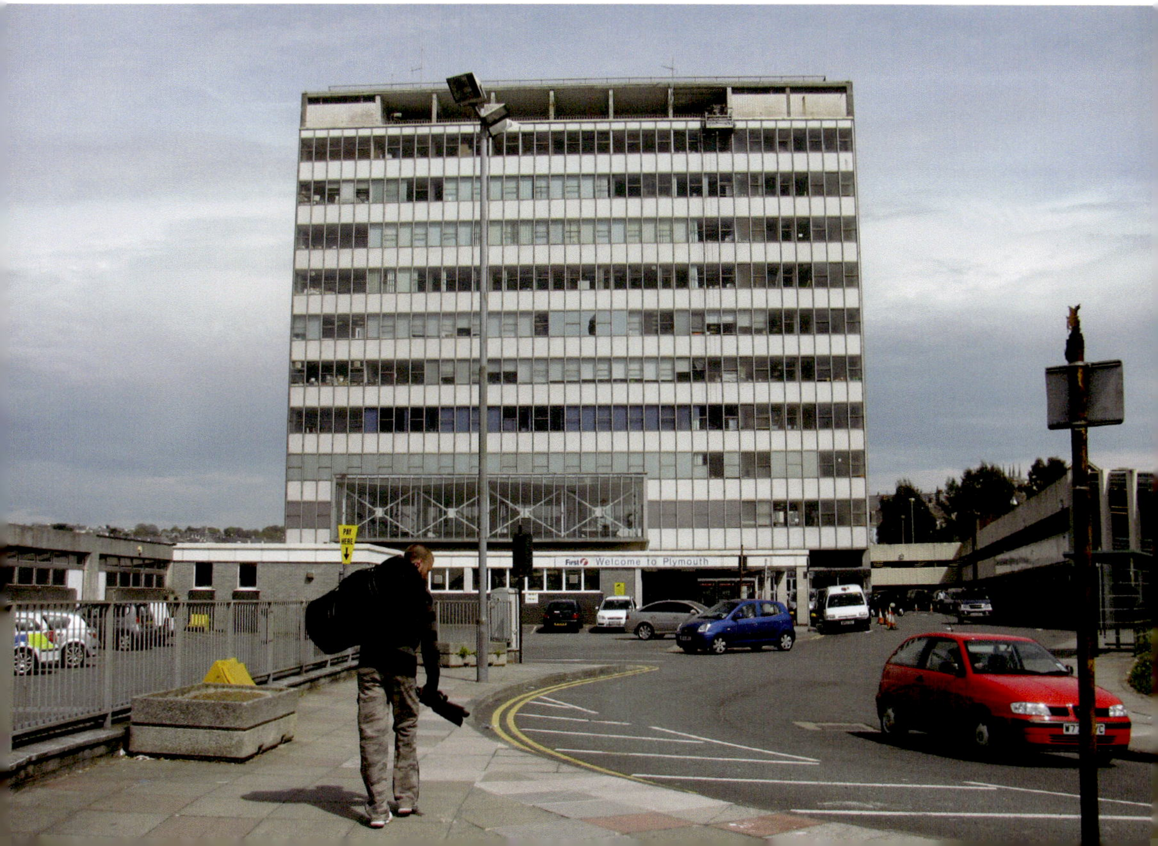

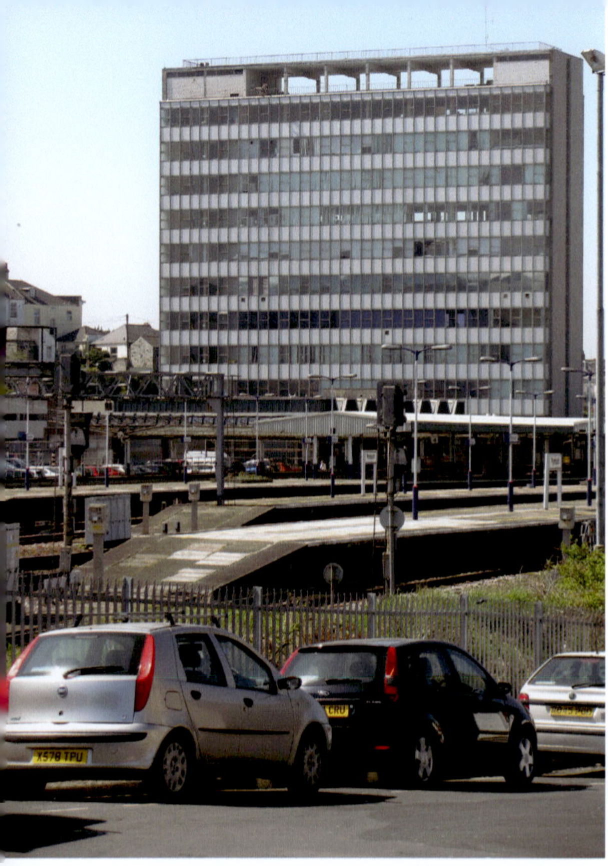

The rear of Intercity House and the platforms at North Road railway station.

Rebuilding work to enlarge the station was planned to start in 1938 but this was interrupted by the Second World War. In 1956, the rebuilding work was resumed using the designs of architects Howard Cavanagh and Ian Campbell. On 26 March 1962, the new station together with its large office block, known as Intercity House, was officially opened by Dr Richard Beeching, the British Railways chairman.

Between 2020 and 2024, the station and the surrounding area went through redevelopment. Intercity Place, the eleven-floor office building adjacent to the station was rebuilt for use by the University of Plymouth. The old car park was demolished and the site is also to be used by the university. A new six-storey car park was built on the site of the former Rail Incident Safety Centre building. Further redevelopment work is due to be completed by 2027.

38. Plymouth Argyle

In 1886, Plymouth Argyle was founded by two friends, F. Howard Grose and W. Pettybridge. Centre-back Grose became the club's first captain. The team had no ground so played their first matches during the 1886–87 season at grounds belonging to their opponents, eventually making their home at a field at Mount Gould.

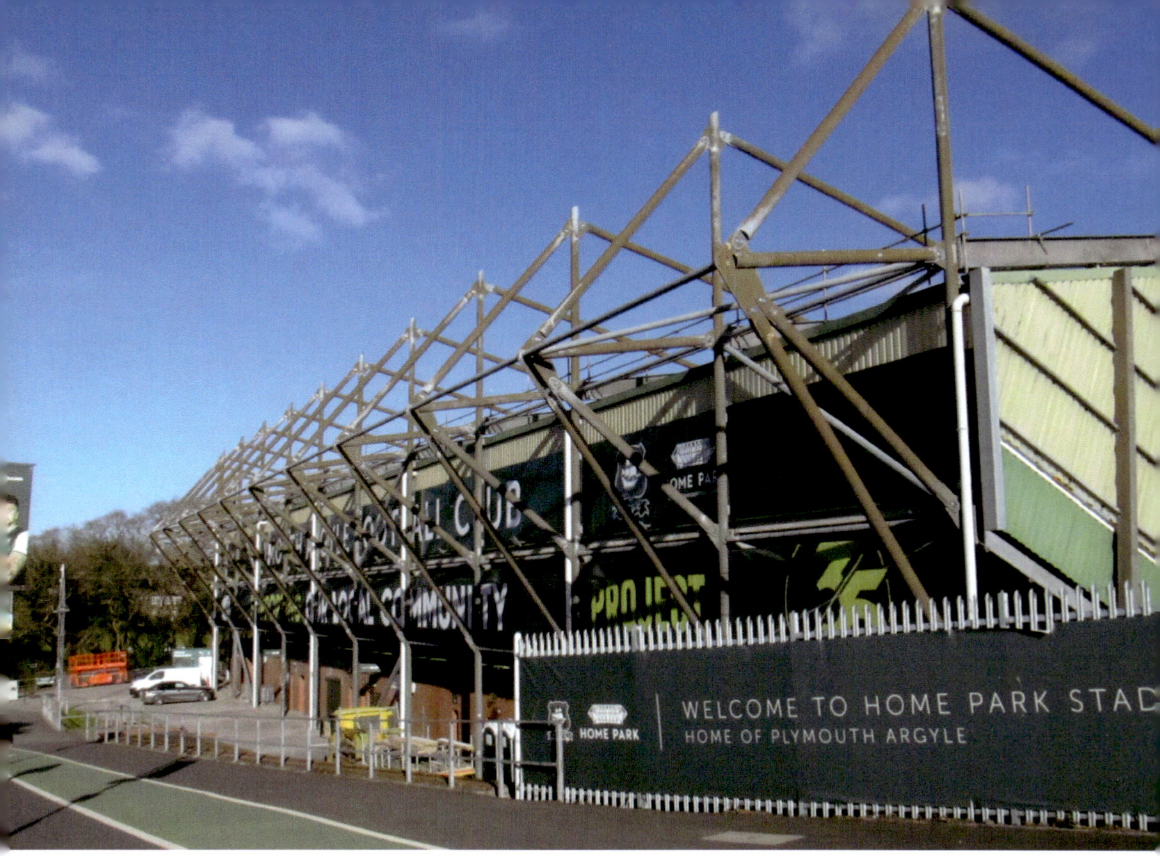

Above: The frontage of Plymouth Argyle's football ground, Home Park.

Below left: The former entrance to Plymouth Argyle, now the club's superstore.

Below right: The scaffold-like frontage of Plymouth Argyle's football ground.

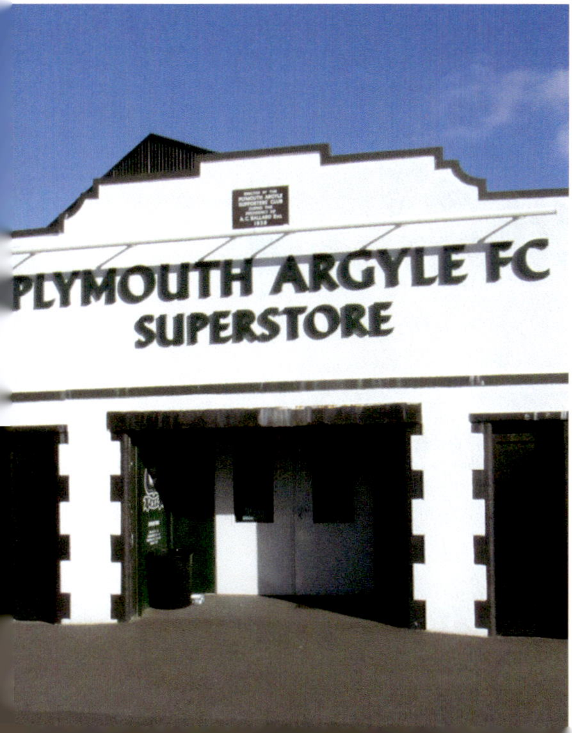

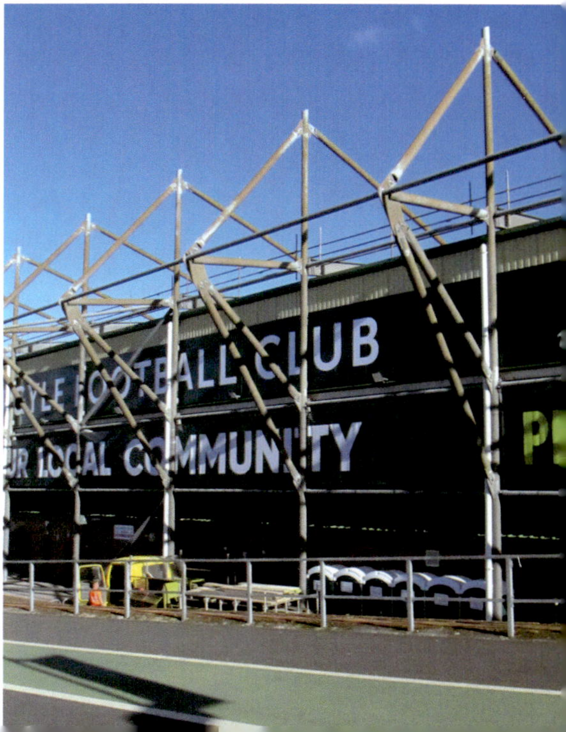

The team's first match was played on 16 October 1886, with Argyle losing 2-0 against Cornish team Caxton. However, their first win came later in the same week when they beat Plymouth College 2-1.

During the 1889–90 season, Argyle found a home at Marsh Mills before moving to their current ground at Home Park in 1901, which had previously belonged to Devonport Albion Rugby Club.

In 1903, Plymouth Argyle became a professional football club with a limited liability company being formed under the watchful eye of local businessman Clarence Spooner.

At the end of the year, the team was accepted into the Southern League, with Frank Brettell becoming their first manager. In their first professional game, they beat West Ham 1-0 and later beat Northampton Town 2-0 when they played their first home game on 5 September 1903, drawing a crowd of 4,438.

During the 1912–13 season, Argyle became Southern League champions and later, in 1920, joined the Football League Division Three (South) under manager Bob Jack, finishing 11th in their first season, with crowd numbers rising to 12,765.

The team won promotion to Football League Division Two during the 1929–30 season, topping Division Three (South), with spectator numbers often reaching 20,000. Matches were put on hold during the Second World War, and the ground was severely damaged by enemy bombing.

At the beginning of the twenty-first century, Argyle's ground, Home Park, was demolished and a new stadium was constructed by Barrs plc, which was completed in May 2002.

At the end of the 2005–06 season, the club bought the stadium from Plymouth City Council for £2.7 million, ending a 125-year lease. However, the stadium was sold back to the council for £16 million in October 2011.

39. The Palace Theatre

The theatre in Union Street was originally called the New Palace Theatre of Varieties and opened in September 1898. The opening show featured Adele and May Lilian, who were billed as the Levey Sisters. They were followed by an acrobatic act called The Six Craggs. Tickets ranged from 1*s* to 2*s* 6*d*.

Fire destroyed both the auditorium and stage during December 1898 and the theatre wasn't opened again until May 1899. There were twice nightly vaudeville shows by 1902 and artists who appeared included Neil Kenyon, a comedian, Robert Williams, a sword swinger, and Miss Gertie Gitana, a singer. In 1909, Houdini played at the theatre and during November 1931, Charlie Chaplin appeared on stage.

The theatre stayed open during the Blitz of 1941 to keep people's spirits up. Acts that appeared that year included Billy Cotton, Tommy Handley and Arthur Lucan. At Christmas, the main show was Robinson Crusoe.

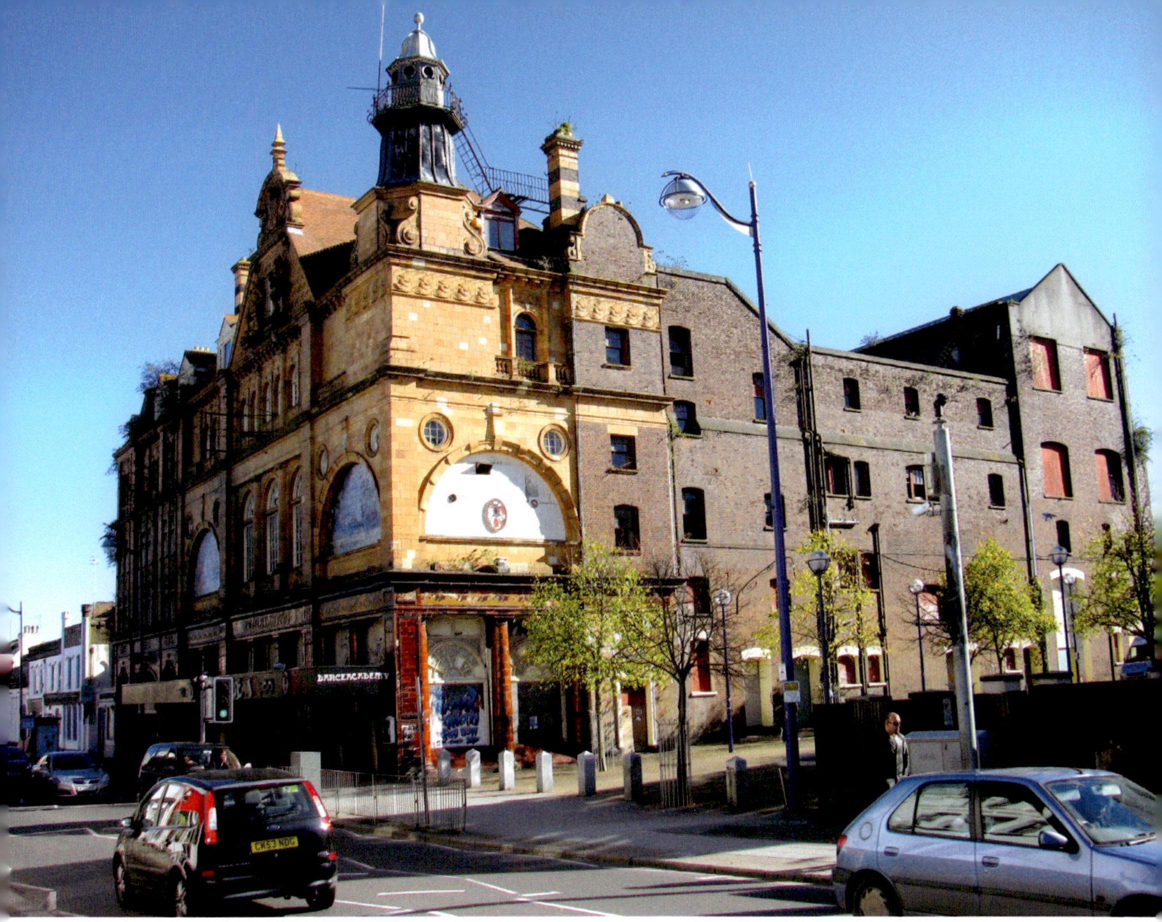

Above: The once grand Palace Theatre in Union Street.

Right: The ornate viewing platform and balcony at the top of the Palace Theatre, now inaccessible.

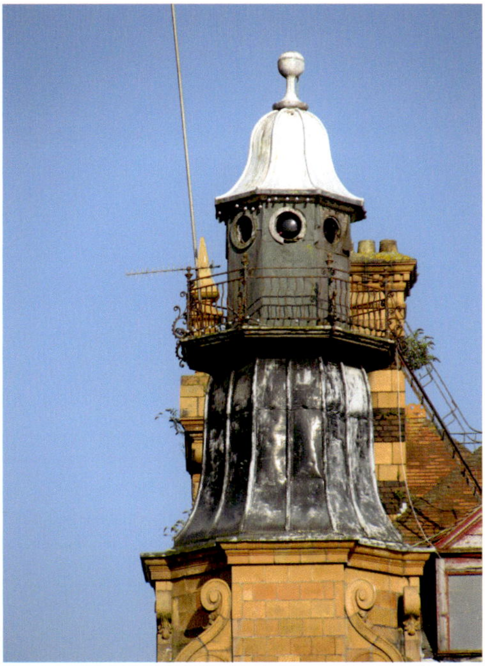

The theatre closed in 1949 for redecorating and reopened with the Billy Cotton Bandshow. The theatre closed again in 1954 due to the lack of touring shows. It was offered to the Plymouth City Council in early 1956 but they refused to buy it and it closed for five months before reopening in October 1956. It closed suddenly on 7 February 1959 during the pantomime *Little Miss Muffet* because of lack of interest.

New management took over the theatre in 1961 and it became Palace Theatre (Bingo) Ltd. The theatre reopened in 1962 with the pantomime *Sinbad the Sailor*. In 1965, Arthur Fox paid £50,000 for the theatre with the intention of hosting Star Bingo, wrestling and striptease.

In 1975, it was bought by EMI and opened on 19 April 1977 with a performance of *The Magic Flute*. The theatre struggled and closed on 27 May 1980. It reopened on 16 May 1981 for a review with Danny La Rue but closed in 1983 and became the Academy.

Its fortunes didn't improve and today it remains closed, its shabby appearance hiding its varied history.

40. The Royal Marine Barracks, Durnford Street

The oldest parts of Stonehouse Barracks date back to 1756. However, the main building work took place between 1779 and 1785 and was undertaken by James Templer and Thomas Parlby. Later buildings were added in the nineteenth century and were designed by Colonel Godfrey Greene.

The front of the Royal Marines' Barracks in Durnford Street.

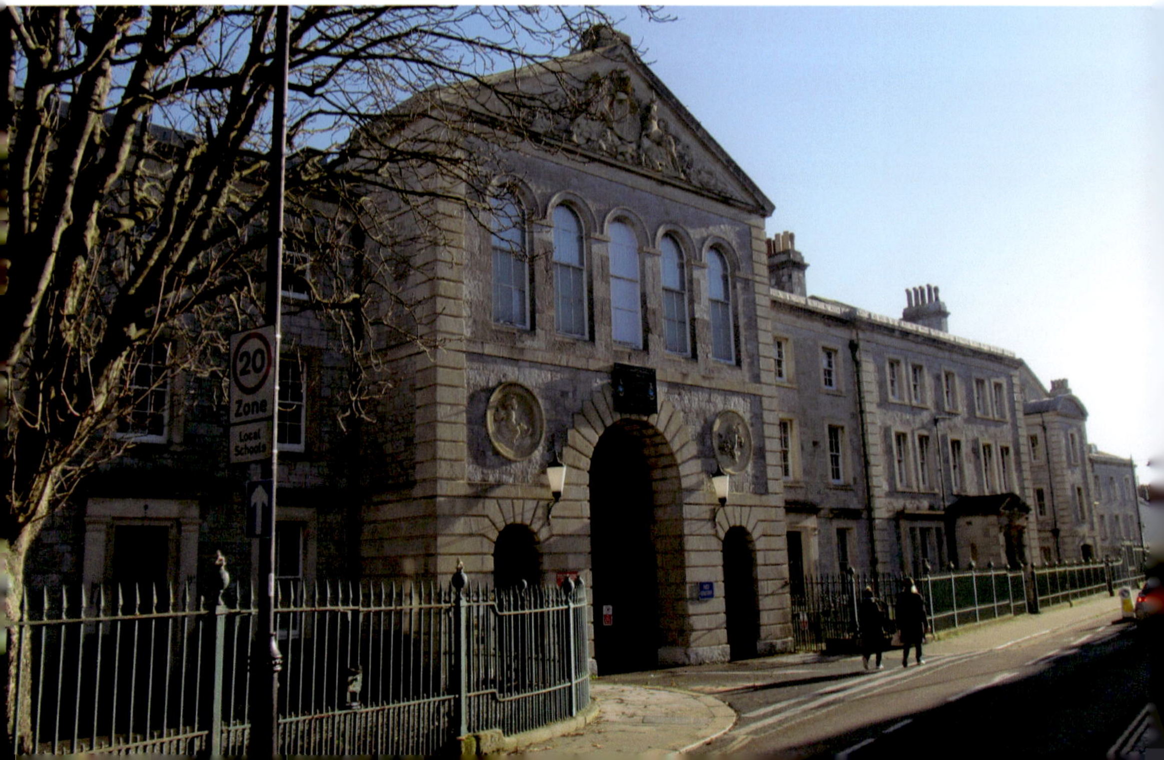

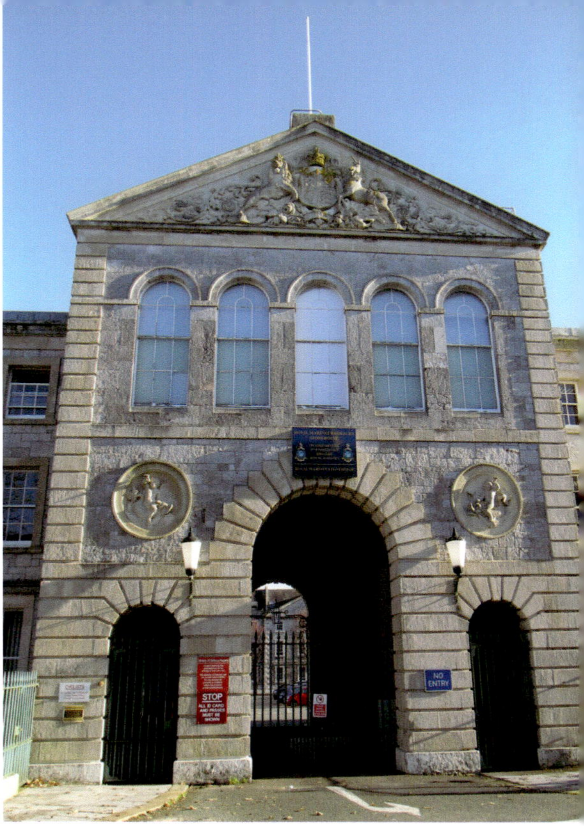

The entrance to the Royal Marines' Barracks.

The original eighteenth-century barracks included a rectangular parade ground together with a symmetrical barrack range on the eastern side, providing accommodation for the privates. A matching pair of shorter officers' barrack blocks stood to the north and south. The commandant and his deputy had houses in the south block, while the north block housed junior officers. The barracks were expanded in the nineteenth century during the Napoleonic Wars and further building work took place during the Crimean War.

The barracks comprise of 454 single accommodation units, as well as two properties for service families, together with training facilities. From 1961 the barracks were home to 43 Commando. The unit disbanded in 1967 but the barracks housed 45 Commando until they moved to RM Condor in 1971.

In 2016, the MOD revealed that it planned to sell the site. However, it was later announced that the barracks would stay operational until 2027. Today, the barracks are the headquarters of 3 Commando Brigade.

41. The Artillery Tower, Firestone Bay

The Artillery Tower at Firestone Bay was constructed during the reign of Henry VIII (1509–47), probably between 1537 and 1539. The blockhouse formed part of a series of coastal defences put in place by Henry VIII. He feared an invasion from the Spanish after he ended his marriage to Catherine of Aragon, the aunt

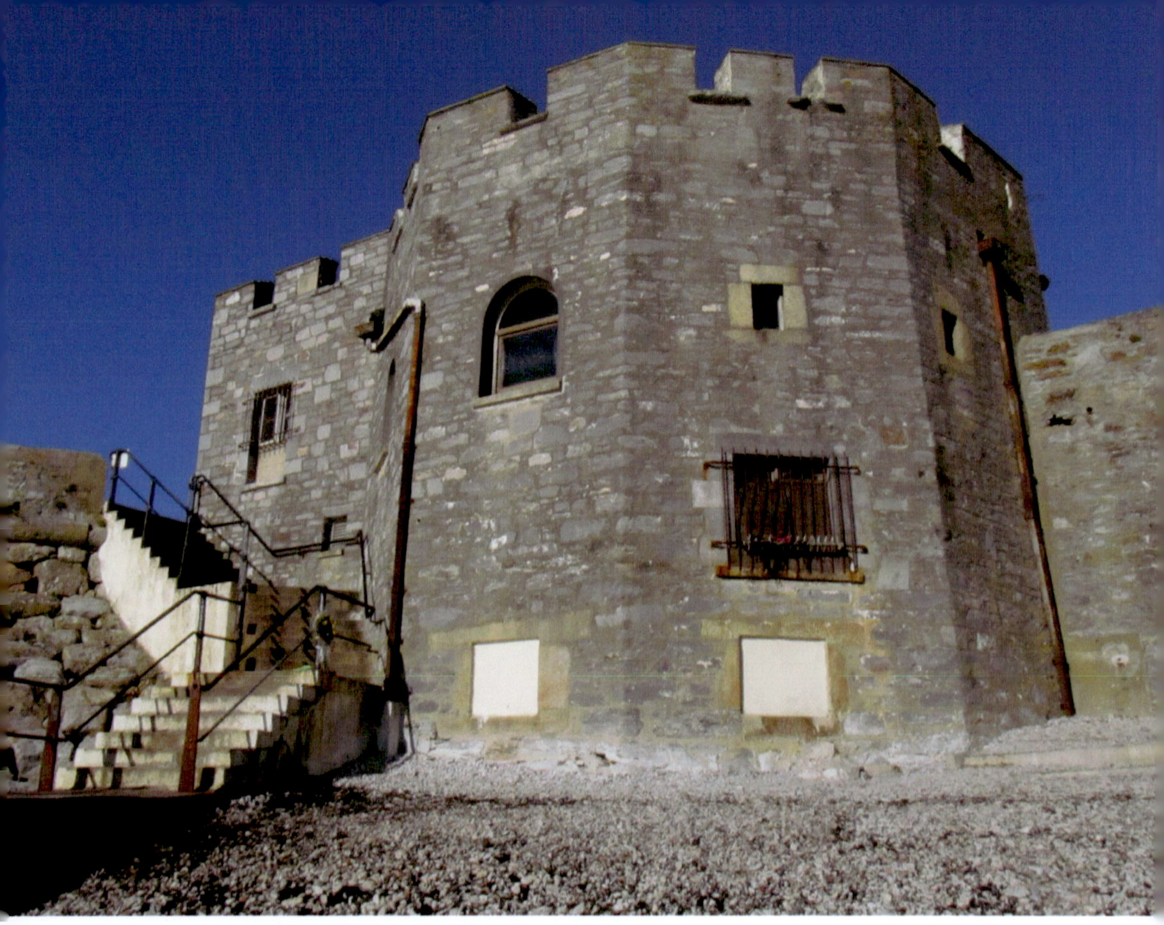

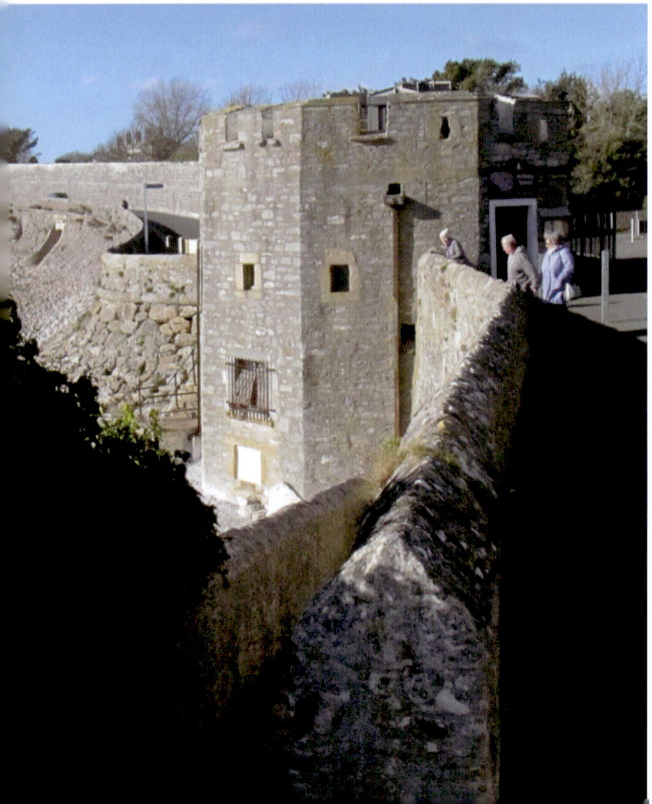

Above: The Artillery Tower at Firestone Bay as seen from the shore below.

Left: The Artillery Tower as seen from above.

to King Charles V of Spain. France and the Empire declared an alliance against Henry in 1538 and the pope encouraged the two countries to launch an attack against England.

The Edgcumbe family had the tower built to defend the harbour from invading forces. The octagonal tower is constructed from rubble and has granite dressings. A parapet originally surrounded the vaulted roof and a number of gun ports face towards the sea. The original doorway still survives, as well as rectangular openings facing the sea. By the gun openings, there are grooves for shutters.

In 1902, a machine gun post was mounted there to protect the harbour boom. Similar towers survive at Devil's Point, Fisher's Nose and Mount Edgcumbe. Further blockhouses stood at Millbay West and Millbay East but they no longer exist.

The blockhouse is a Schedule Monument and is Grade II listed. Today, the building houses the Artillery Tower Restaurant.

42. Royal William Yard

Work commenced on the Royal William Victualling Yard in 1826. It was designed by Sir John Rennie to be used by the Admiralty as a victualling base for the Royal Navy. The whole site covered an area of 16 acres, including 6 acres of land that were recovered from the sea. It was originally intended for it to be named after King George IV but he died in 1830 of cirrhosis and dropsy and instead the yard was named after his successor, William, who was sixty-four when he came to the throne. He laid the coping stone of the sea wall while he was the Duke of Clarence and the Clarence Block and the Clarence Steps recognise this.

The cost of the yard was approximately £2 million and it was completed in 1835. By then, the Duke of Clarence had succeeded to the throne and had become King William IV. By order of the Admiralty in 1833, it was named the Royal William Victualling Yard after William IV, who was the last Lord High Admiral.

A statue of King William IV stands over the grand entrance of the yard in Cremyll Street. The statue stands 13 feet 9 inches and is surrounded by sculptures of the trades that were once incorporated within the yard including bakers, coopers and butchers.

The yard continued to be used by the navy until 1992 when it was sold off. In April 1993, the yard became open to the public. Clarence, the oldest and main building on the site, was redeveloped into fifty-two apartments. Previously, it had been used to store spirits, beer and vinegar. The brewhouse was turned into seventy-eight apartments with cafés, restaurants and exhibition space on the ground floor.

Today, the yard is well visited and the work to develop the older parts into useful premises continues.

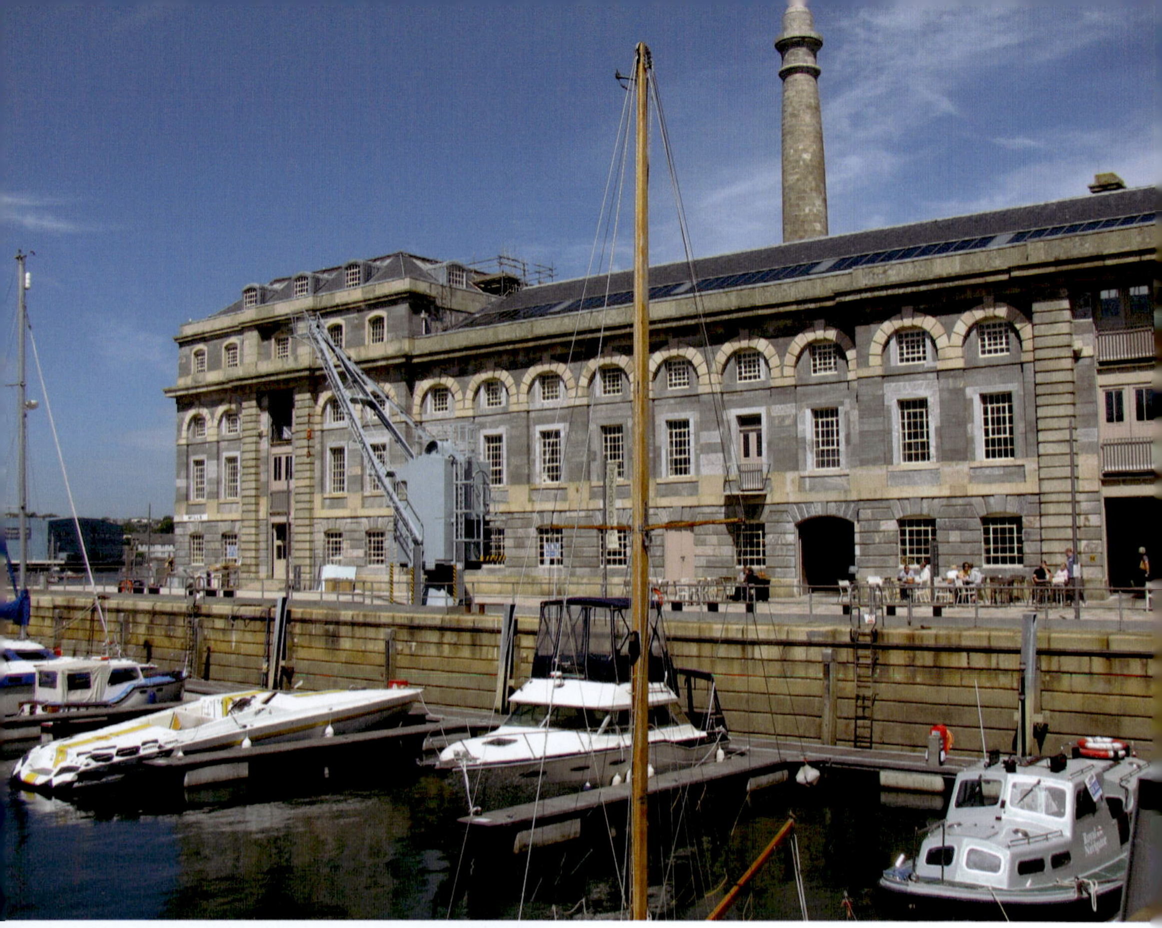

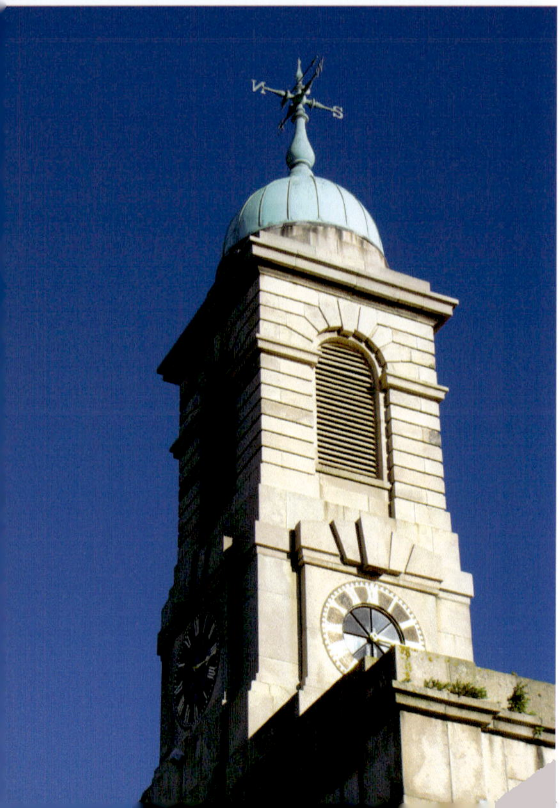

Above: The richly decorated buildings within Royal William Yard, mostly eateries, galleries and accommodation.

Left: The clock tower within Royal William Yard.

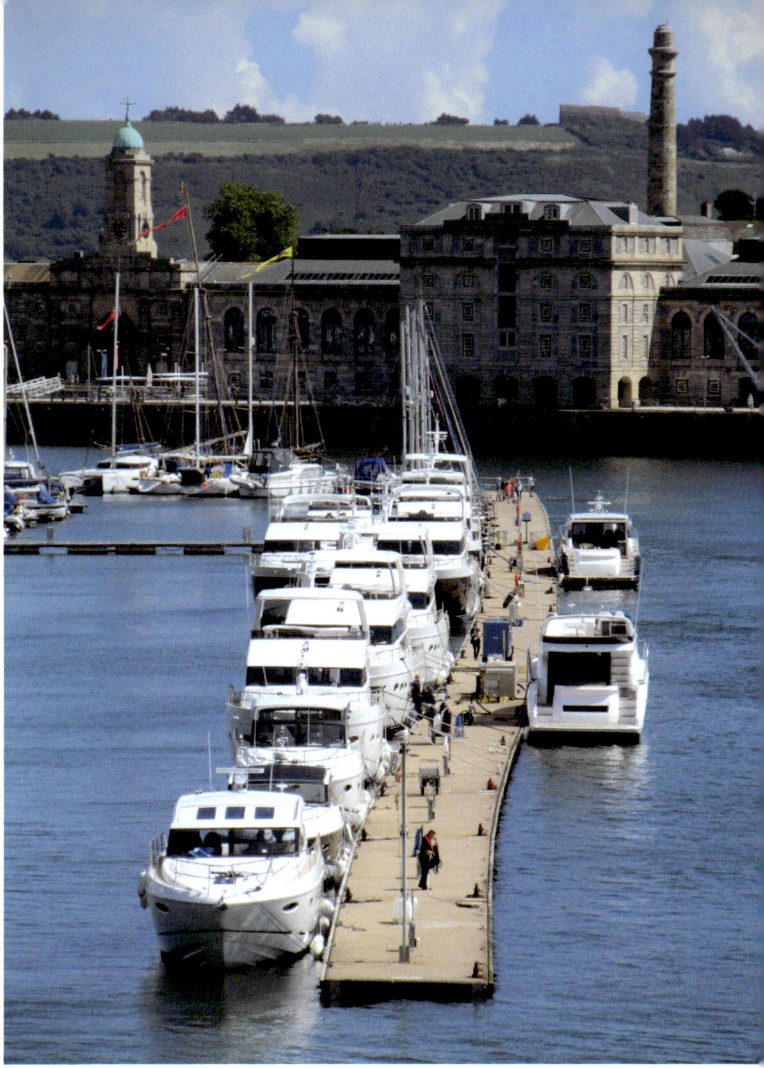

Looking towards Royal William Yard from Mount Wise.

43. St Peter and the Holy Apostles Church, Stonehouse

Wyndham Square was developed in the 1830s as part of John Foulston's major development of the area between Plymouth and Stonehouse. Originally, the square surrounded a Nonconformist chapel, which was replaced by St Peter's Church, built between 1880 and 1882. The church was built using limestone in an Early English style. It features a Lady Chapel, south porch and a copper-capped western tower. The spire was completed in 1906.

Terraces were built to the north and south of the square. Densham Terrace was completed by 1848, followed by the development of the east side of Cecil Street. St Peter's was extensively damaged in the Second World War during the Blitz and was later rebuilt by Frederick Etchells in 1955 and was reconsecrated in 1956. Between 2004 and 2007, the church was renovated with impressive results. Princess Margaret was patron of the restoration fund and a stained-glass window

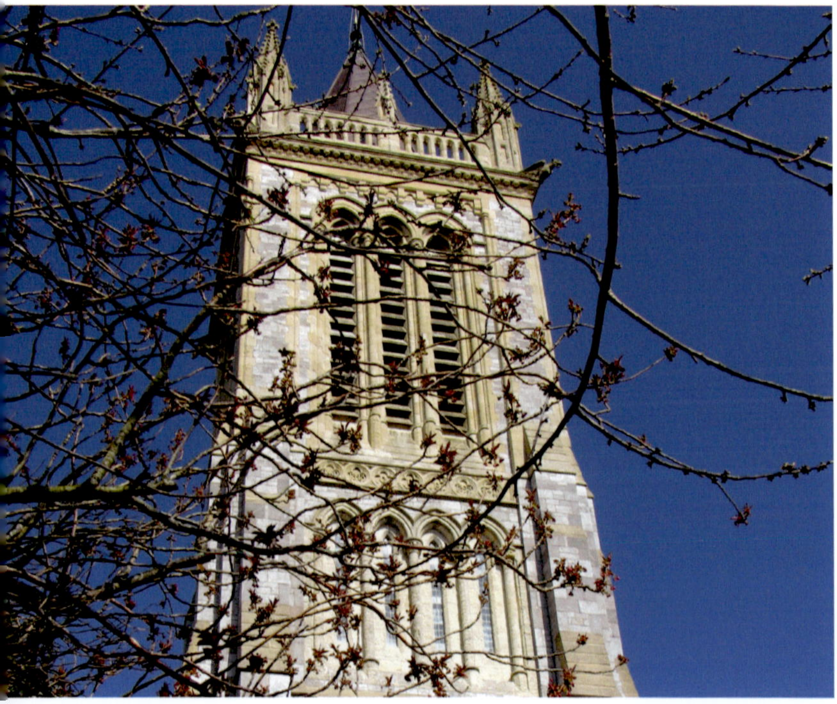

The ornate tower of St Peter and the Holy Apostles Church in Stonehouse.

Below left: St Peter and the Holy Apostles Church and Wyndham Square.

Below right: The rear of St Peter and the Holy Apostles Church from Wyndham Street East.

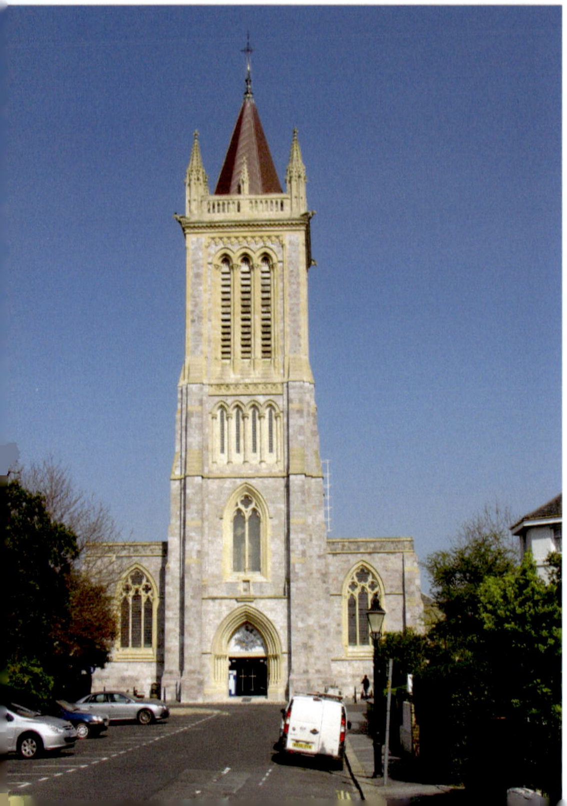

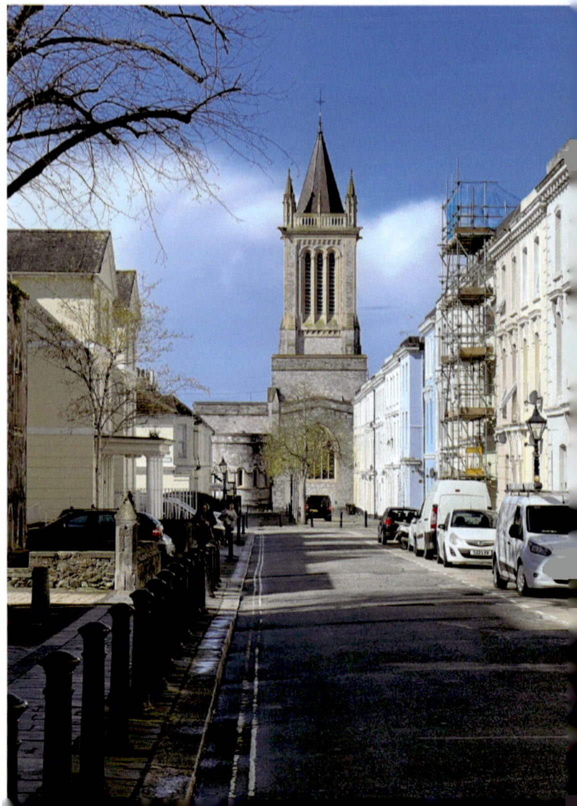

is displayed in her memory. The windows were designed by local artist James Paterson.

Many of the nearby properties are Grade II listed and, during the last century, some were reported to be haunted.

44. The Old Chapel, Devonport

Work on the Old Chapel in George Street began in 1790 and it was opened in April 1791. It served as a Nonconformist Unitarian chapel for what was then known as Plymouth Dock. In 1791, three Unitarians were executed in Birmingham for their part in a riot there. Commissioner Fanshaw stated that any workers within the dockyard who attended the chapel would be dismissed as disloyal subjects. Because of the ruling, attendance was low and the chapel struggled. The chapel closed fifteen years after it opened.

It was converted into a public house in the early 1800s and remained in business until the mid-1990s. For a while in the early 1900s, it was used as a wine and spirit store and belonged to Messrs A. & C. Barnes.

The front of the Old Chapel in Devonport, now a Co-op.

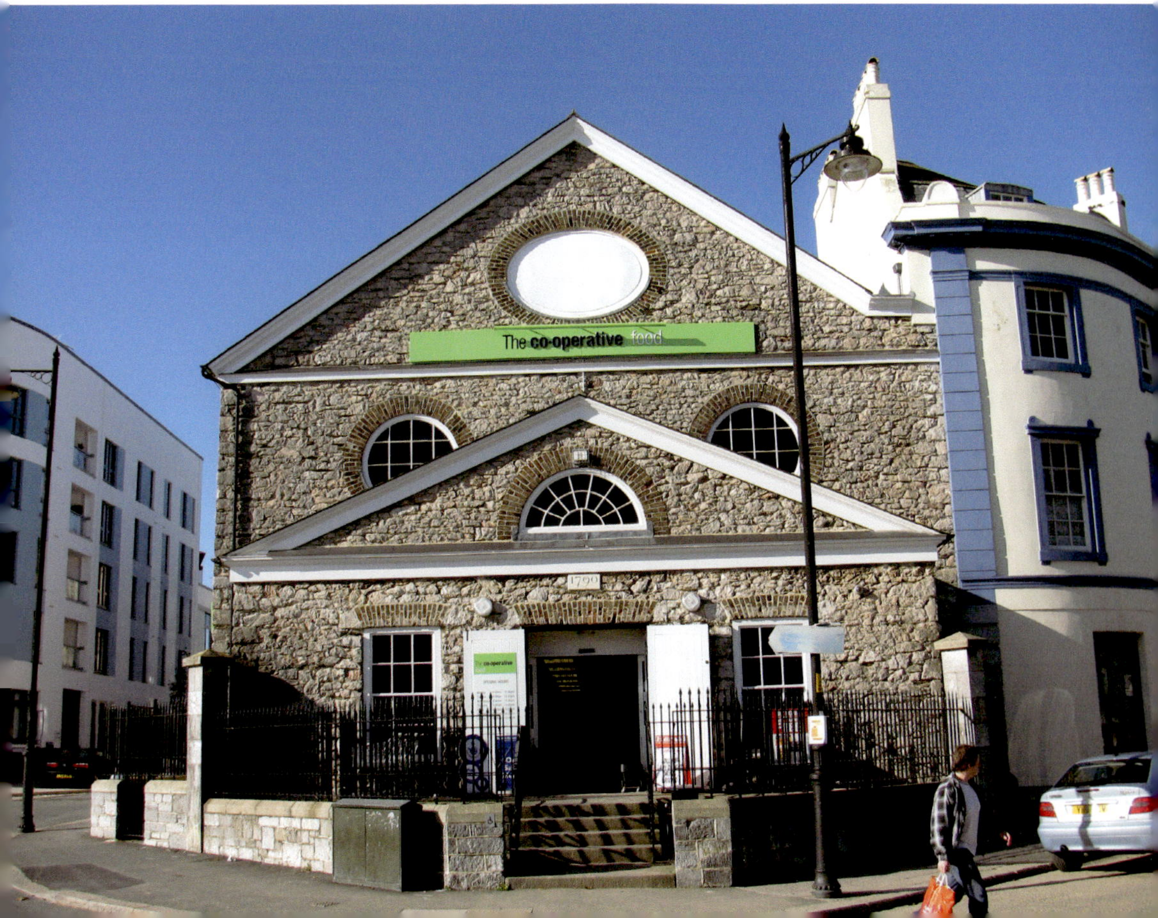

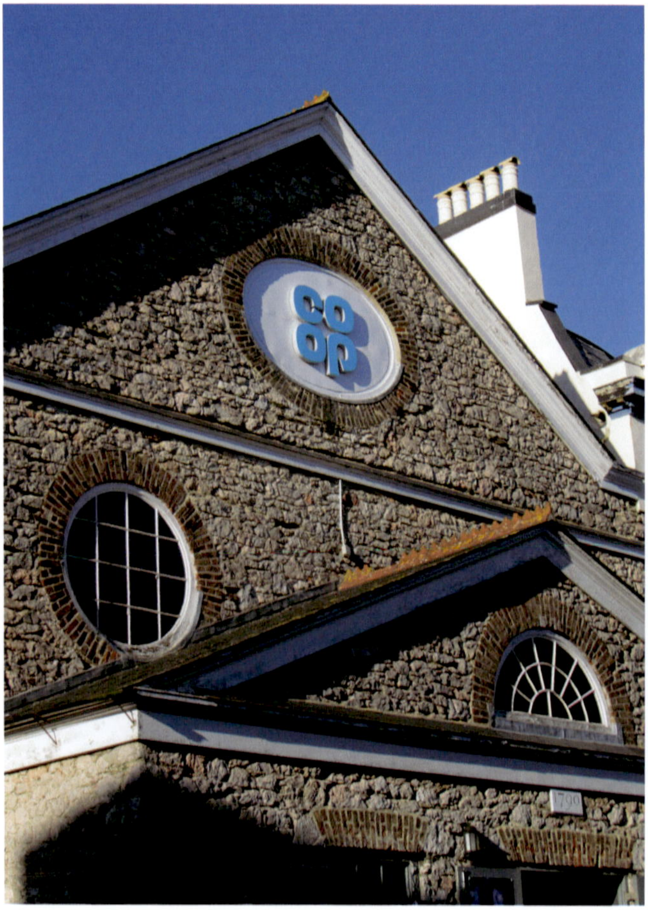

Looking towards the upper part of the Old Chapel with new signage.

The congregation continued to meet secretly until they re-established themselves in 1820. In 1829, they opened the Granby Street Unitarian Chapel.

The building fell into a state of disrepair in the later 1990s but was refurbished and reopened as a Co-operative convenience store in 2000. It had previously been listed as a Grade II building in 1954.

45. Devonport Guildhall

The Guildhall was designed by John Foulston and completed between 1821 and 1824 as a copy of the Parthenon in Greece. It was designed in the Regency style with Greek Doric features. Foulston designed a collection of four buildings nearby, which included the Guildhall, the Column, the Mount Zion Calvinist Chapel and the Oddfellow's Hall. Three still stand but the chapel no longer exists. The guildhall was built by a Mr Richard, who also later constructed the nearby victory column.

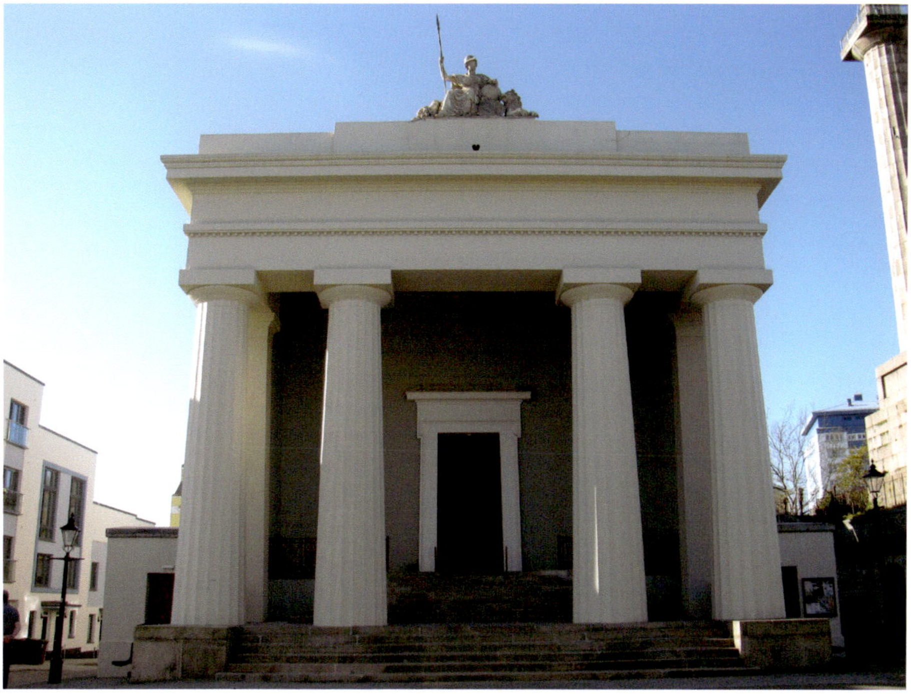

Above: The grand frontage of the Devonport Guildhall in Ker Street.

Below left: Looking through the towers of the Devonport Guildhall towards the Egyptian House.

Below right: The imposing towers of Devonport Guildhall together with a sculpture of Britannia.

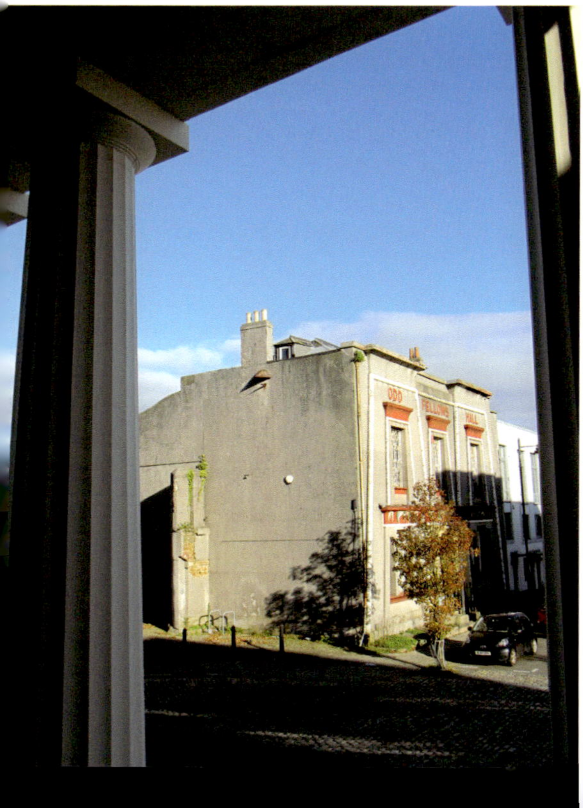

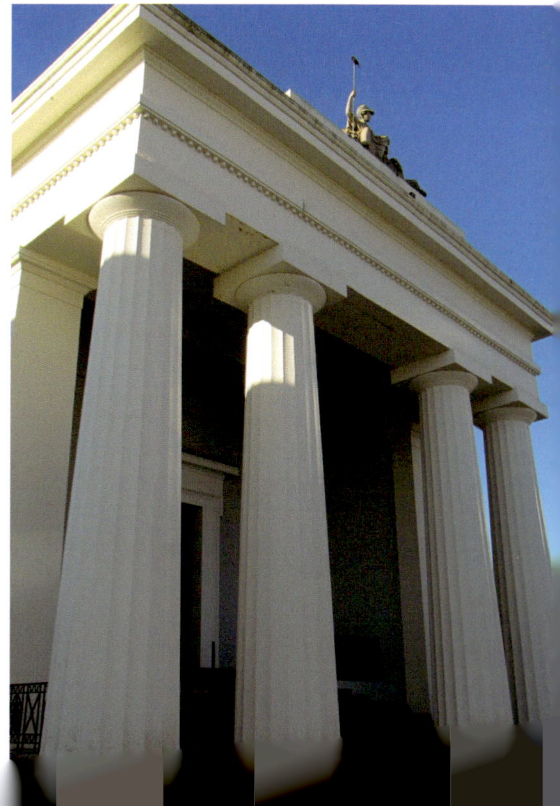

The guildhall housed the magistrates' court and the Mayor's Parlour. It was also used for social events. Fixtures in the courtroom were removable so that events and balls could be held in the evening. The guildhall also included cells and a mortuary. At the rear of the building was a police station.

When Devonport, Stonehouse and Plymouth amalgamated in 1914, the building fell into disrepair. Municipal functions were transferred to the heart of Plymouth. However, the building still had a purpose and was utilised often. It was a gas-mask collection point during the Second World War and Christmas parties for children were held there in the 1940s.

The building became neglected but in 1986, it opened as a Citizens' Advice Bureau, a library, a playgroup, café and sports hall. The building proved too large to maintain and failed to survive.

In 2009, a £1.75 million Community Assets Grant was awarded to the Real Ideas Organisation, who restored the guildhall to its former glory. They worked closely with Plymouth City Council, as well as with the former Devonport Regeneration Community Partnership with the local community in mind. The building was repainted, restored and reopened in 2010.

Today, the guildhall is used as a wedding venue, hosts various events and is used for community activity. The nearby Column was also renovated by Real Ideas and was reopened in 2013. It has stunning views across the city from a viewing platform 124 feet up.

The guildhall is Grade I listed.

46. The Egyptian House

The Odd Fellows Hall can be found at the top of Ker Street near the Devonport Column and Guildhall. It was designed by John Foulston and was built in 1823. At that time, it was more popularly known as the Egyptian House. There is another similar Egyptian-style house in Penzance which has three floors, whereas this one in Devonport only has two. On the front of the building is a plaque that reads 'EGYPTIAN HOUSE'. It was designed in the Egyptian style following the popularisation of Egyptian architecture after the Napoleonic campaigns, one of only two such examples in the country. 'JOHN FOULSTON 1823'.

The first occupier of the building was the Stonehouse and Devonport Classical and Mathematical Subscription School. In 1827, it was bought by the Civil and Military Library, who opened it as a public library and newsroom. In 1867, the building was sold to the Odd Fellows Society, who, for a time, leased it to the Mount Zion Congregation. However, the building stayed in the hands of the Odd Fellows for almost 100 years before being purchased in 1968 by Tony Cooper, the owner of the nearby Forum in Fore Street, who turned it into a social club.

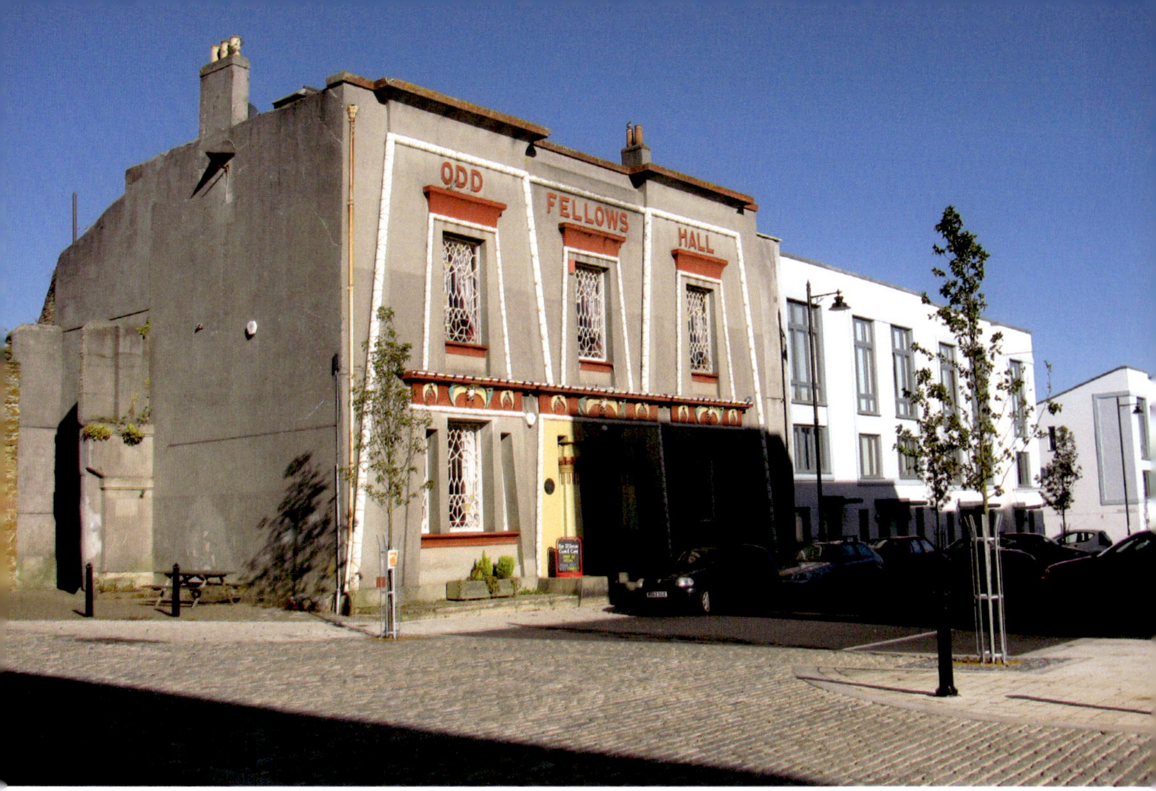

Above: Looking towards the Egyptian House in Ker Street.

Right: The highly decorated frontage of the Egyptian House.

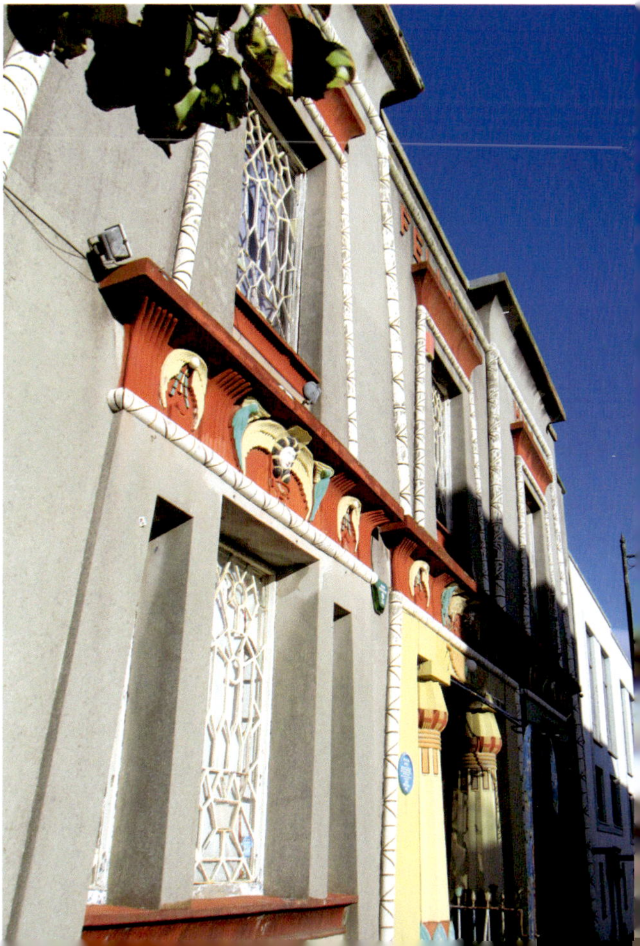

47. The Forum, Devonport

The Forum Cinema was opened on 5 August 1939 and formed part of the very busy Fore Street in Devonport. The premises had previously belonged to Messrs Swiss & Company, who sold the building to Devonport Kinemas Ltd of No. 10 Windsor Place, Cardiff. The new cinema building was designed by E. C. Morgan Willmott & Partners Ltd, also of Cardiff. The new cinema contained 1,800 seats and had a frontage of 75 feet and was 130 feet in length. Construction work was undertaken by Charles Tyler, of Swansea, Glamorgan, South Wales. The cinema was run jointly with the nearby Hippodrome and both had the same licensee, A. E. Taylor, and manager, W. G. Thomas.

The first movie shown was *Honolulu*, which starred Eleanor Powell and Robert Young. In the main part of the cinema, seats cost *6d*, *9d* or 1*s*, whilst on the balcony, the cost was 1*s* 3*d* and 1*s* 6*d*.

The whole area changed dramatically during April 1941 due to enemy bombing. The Forum Cinema suffered damage while the nearby picture houses, the Electric Cinema, the Tivoli Cinema and the Hippodrome, were completely destroyed. The Forum closed for a short period while it was being repaired. The face of Fore

The front of the Forum Cinema in Fore Street, Devonport, when it was still a bingo hall.

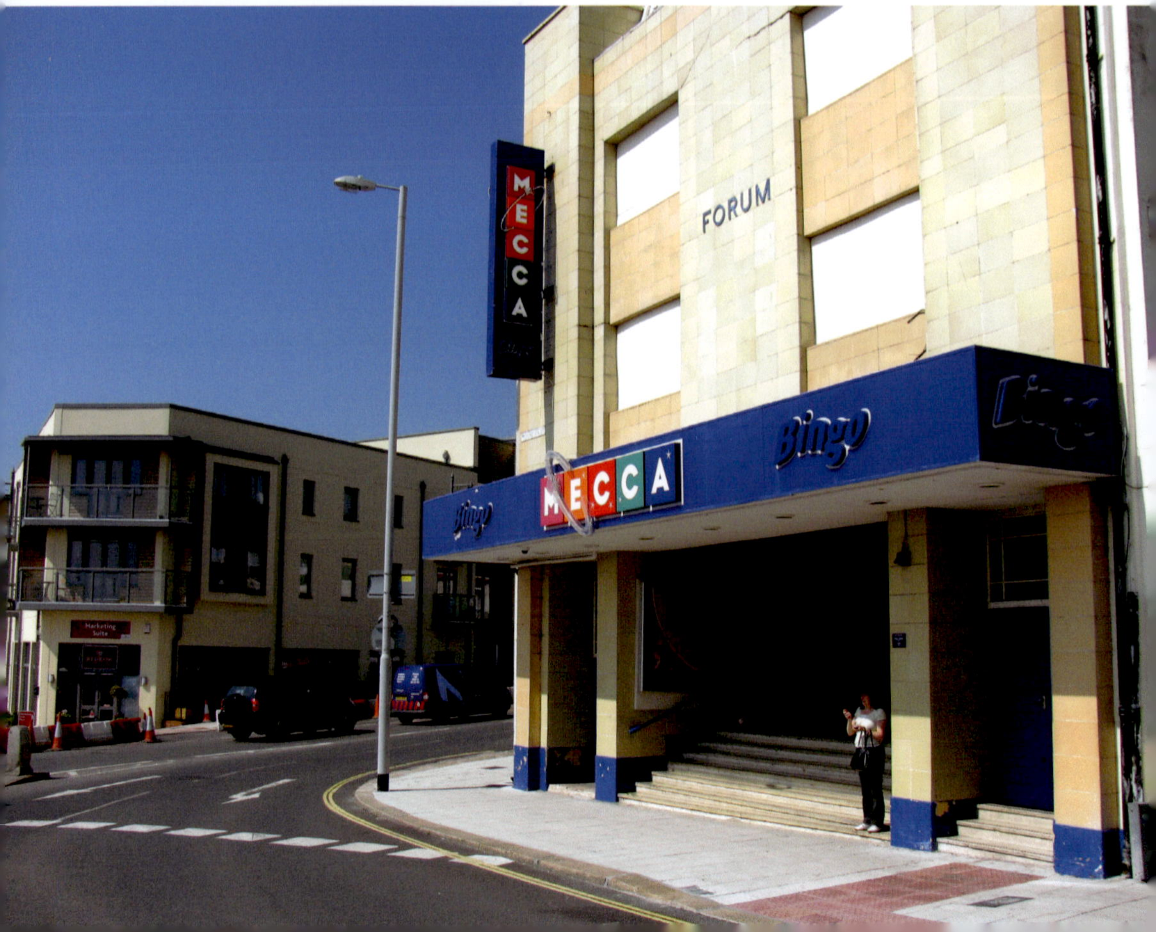

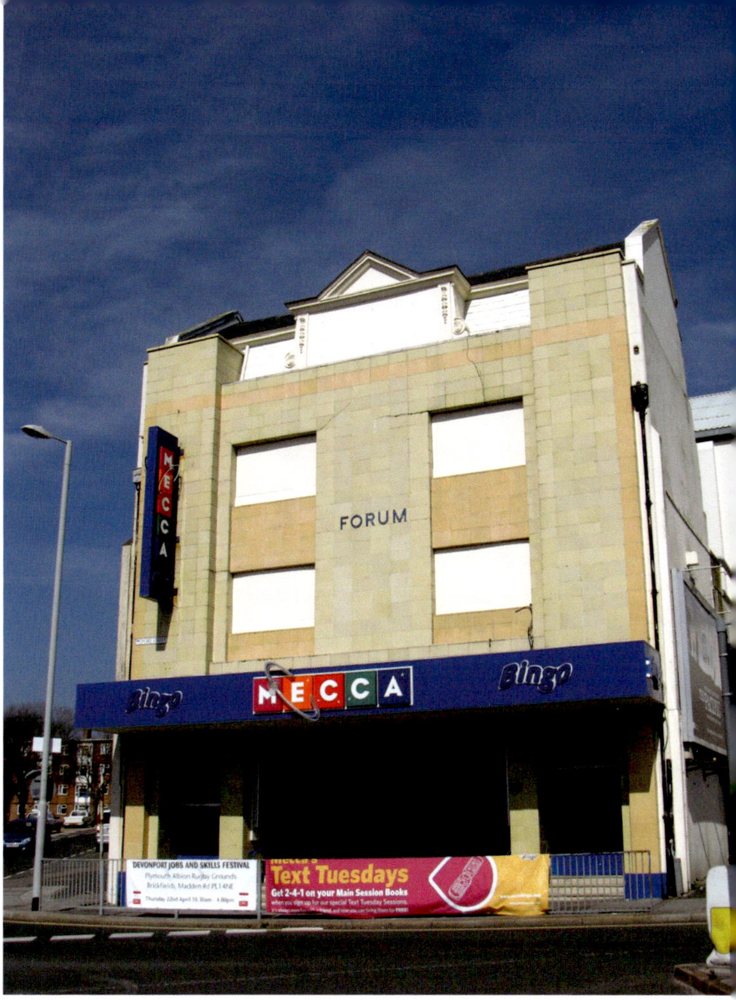

The Forum once stood in a very busy street with many adjoining shops. However, much was destroyed in the Second World War.

Street changed completely with the bottom half being taken over by the Admiralty and enclosed in the dockyard.

In the mid-1950s, the cinema was equipped with CinemaScope. However, it closed as a cinema on 14 May 1960 and was converted into a Mecca bingo hall in December 1960. The advent of television and the face of Devonport changing forever due to war damage meant that there were less people nearby visiting the picture house. It was later taken over by Top Rank and remained a bingo hall. In the late 2000s, it became a Mecca bingo hall again. It proved very popular for many years but eventually closed for good.

Today, the building is empty and looks worse for wear and there seems to be no plans to reopen it.

48. The Swiss Cottage, Devonport

The Swiss Lodge and Devonport Park were renovated several years ago but for many years, the lodge lay in a state of disrepair. It was designed by Alfred

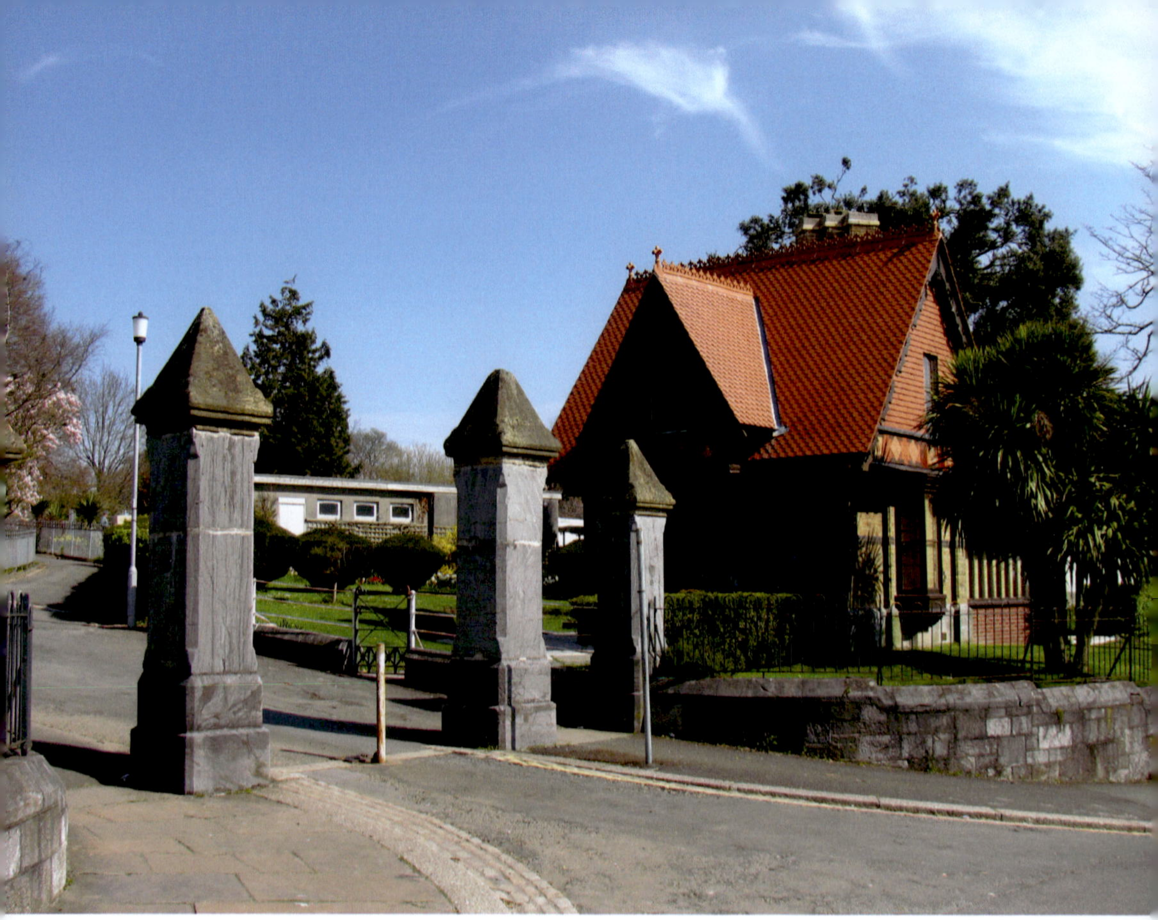

Above: The Swiss Lodge at the entrance to Devonport Park in Fore Street.

Opposite: The rear of the Swiss Lodge, as seen when leaving the park.

Norman of Devonport and built in 1858. Also known as Lower Lodge, it is positioned at the entrance at Fore Street, once one of the main tram routes. The lodge was extended in the early 1900s. It features polychrome buff-coloured brick with blue brick dressings and a clay plain tile roof. The building was Grade II listed in 2000. The land was originally owned by the military and used for army training.

Devonport Park was opened to the public in 1895. Alfred Norman also designed other structures within the park and Messrs Arnold & Son and George Perkins were responsible for the construction work. Just yards away from the lodge is Napier Fountain, which was erected in 1863 in memory of Admiral Sir Charles Napier (1787–1860). Other major features within the park include the Great War Memorial, which was erected in 1923; the Sicilian Fountain in the rose garden near to Higher Lodge; the Doris Gun, which was captured in the Boer War; the Higher Lodge, once a two-storey refreshment pavilion, now a residential home; and the Chatham Vase, located north of Lower Lodge, which commemorates famous Britons who opposed the Spanish.

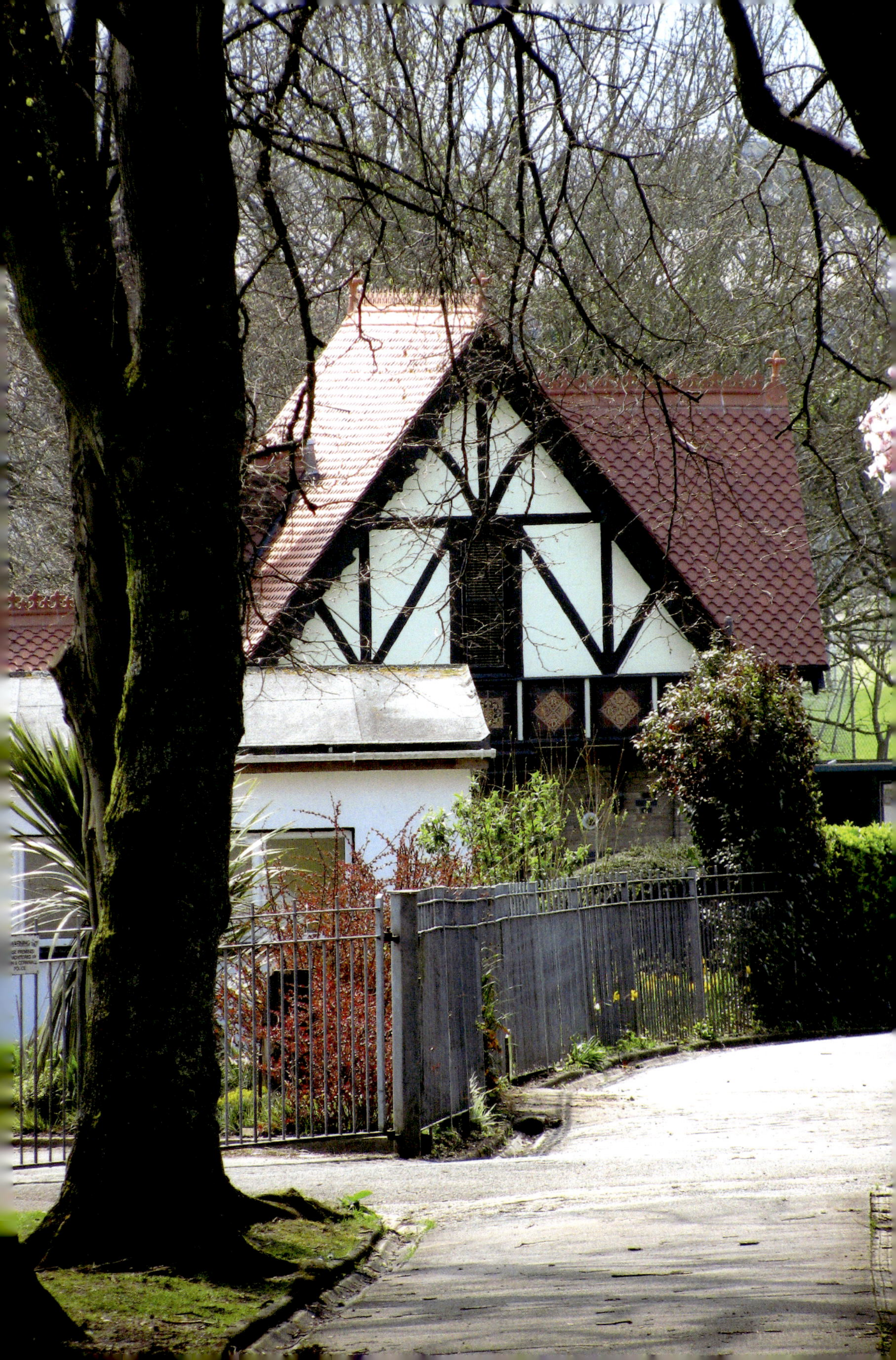

The park also features a bandstand. An ornate bandstand stood in the park for many years before being demolished. It had regularly been used by Devonport's military bands and listening to music in the park in the afternoon proved very popular. The bandstand was replaced in recent years after the park received a £3.3 million grant from the lottery fund. The new bandstand was officially opened in 2012. For many years, the park had been in general decline but the formation of the Friends of Devonport Park in 2005 made sure that the park was maintained and restored and today is very well kept and an interesting place to visit.

49. Devonport Technical School

In 1893, Devonport's Technical Instruction Committee took out a five-year lease on a building at No. 38 George Street to be used as a location for a new technical school. By October, 425 students had registered to attend the school. However, the premises were found to be inadequate and land was required from the War Department so that the Technical School could be built and a loan from the local governing board for £14,000 was acquired to complete the works.

The Devonport Technical School in Paradise Road, now luxury accommodation.

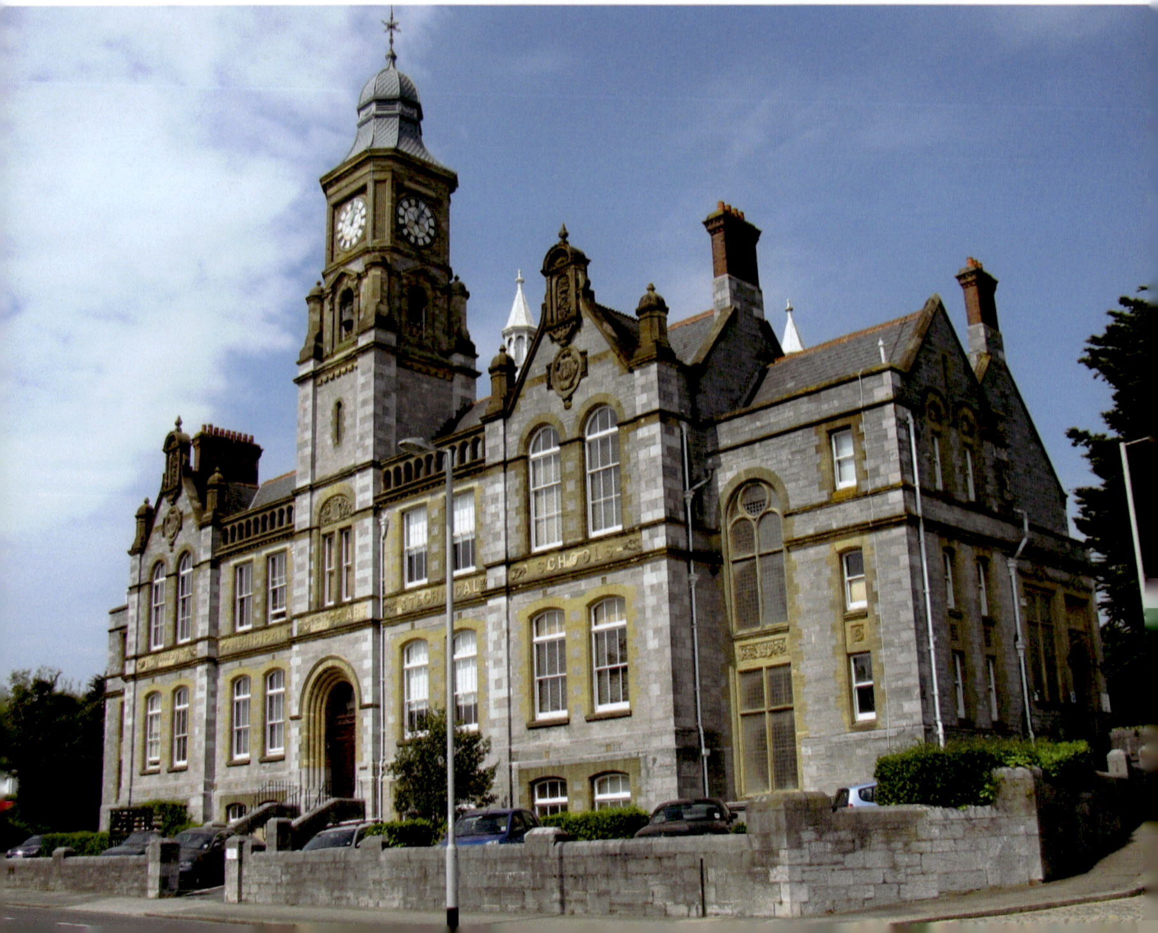

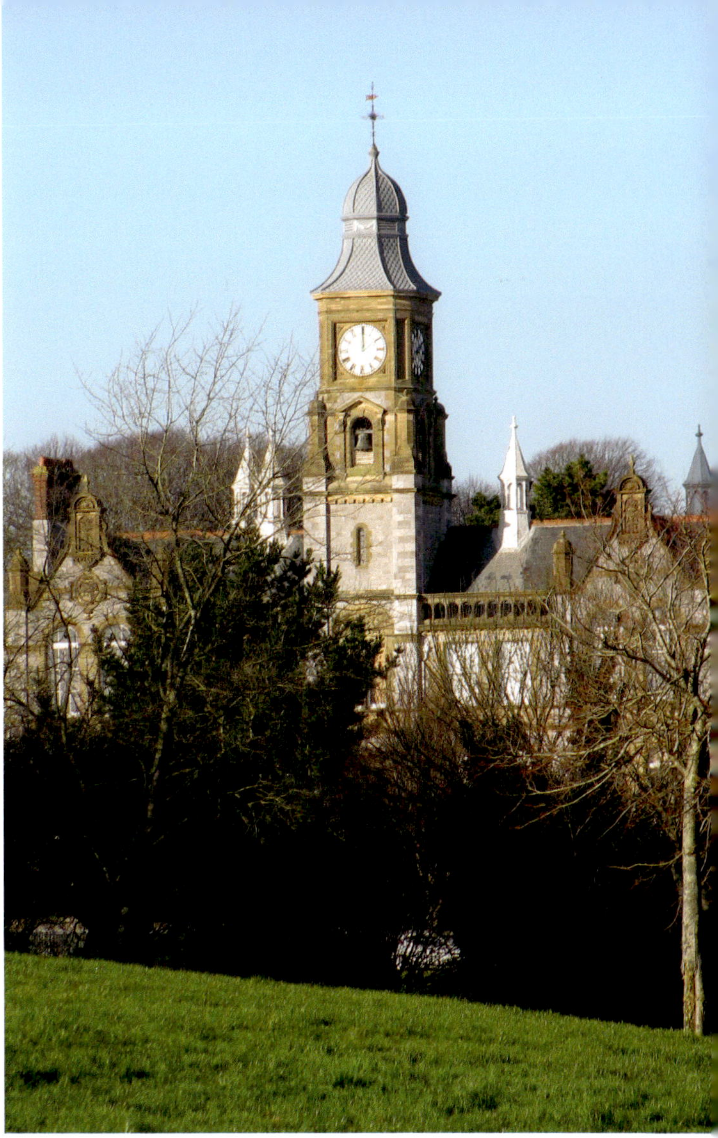

The clock tower of the old Devonport Technical School.

The Mayor of Devonport, Mr W. J. Waycott JP, lay the foundation stone on 22 June 1897, the day of Queen Victoria's Diamond Jubilee. The building was designed by architect Henry Snell and was built by Thomas May of Cobourg Street, Plymouth.

The Technical College was opened on 25 July 1899 by the then Mayor William Hornbrook. It included classrooms, a lecture room and workshops for students to learn a trade. Messrs Fouracre of East Stonehouse provided a stained-glass window which stood in the north wall opposite the mail entrance. The window depicted the development of naval architecture during the career of Sir William White, who had started as a dockyard apprentice and had risen to the position of Director of Naval Construction. White was elected a Freeman of the Borough on the opening day. The window was presented by the Mayor, Mr William Hornbrook. The clock and chimes in the tower were presented by Alderman John Bright James.

The basement included areas for mechanical engineering, woodwork, a clay-modelling room, a plumbers' workshop, as well as the engine and boiler room for the building. The college's caretaker had a small flat there also.

The ground floor had five classrooms, as well as a large lecture hall that was also a room for technical drawing, a committee room and the office of the college's secretary.

From 1898 until 1936, the building also housed the Devonport Municipal Secondary School for Girls. It became an annexe to the nearby College of Further Education but closed in 1990. It was later developed into luxury apartments.

50. St Budeaux Parish Church

In AD480, Budoc, the Bishop of Dol, sailed across from Brittany to the south English coast and landed his craft in an inlet off the River Tamar. This inlet is believed to be at Tamerton Creek. A crude stone cross was erected by him in Ernesettle Woods and a chapel was built near to Warren Point. The original

The entrance to the church at Higher St Budeaux where Francis Drake married Mary Newman.

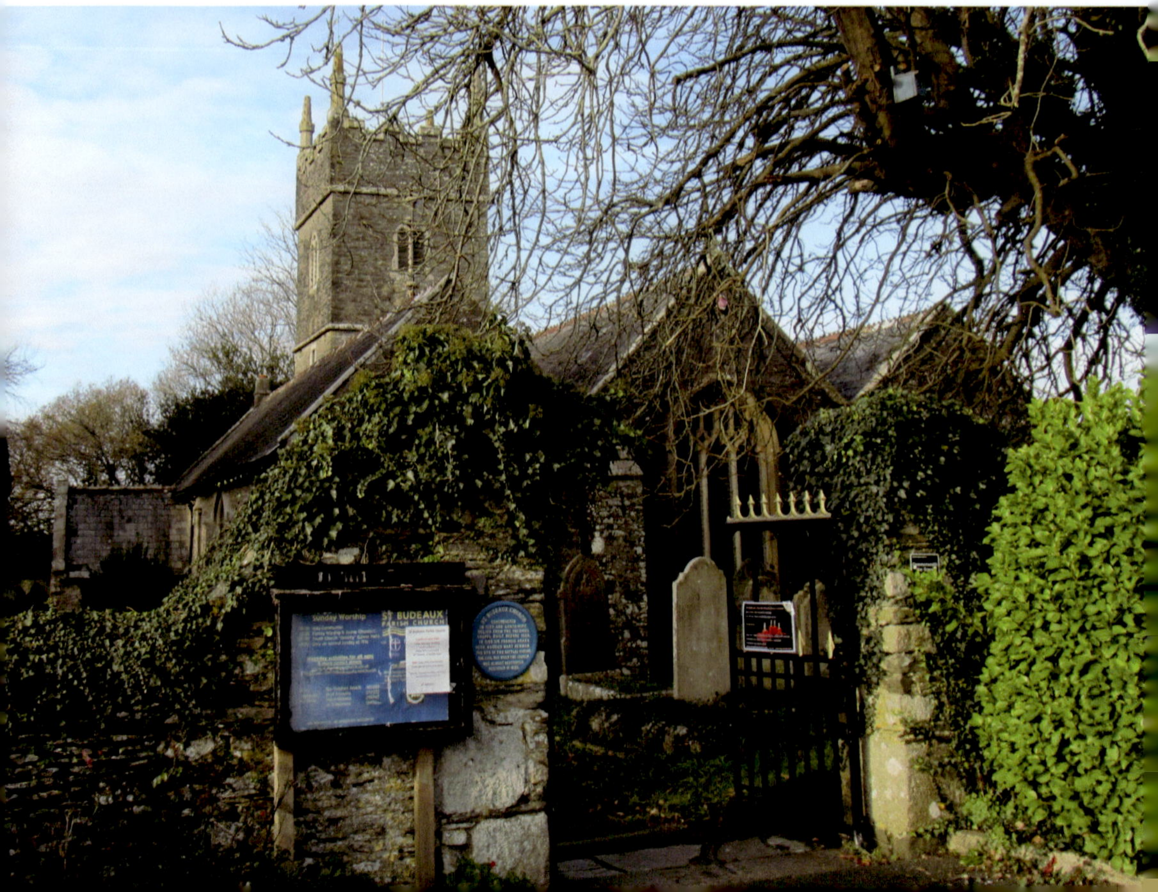

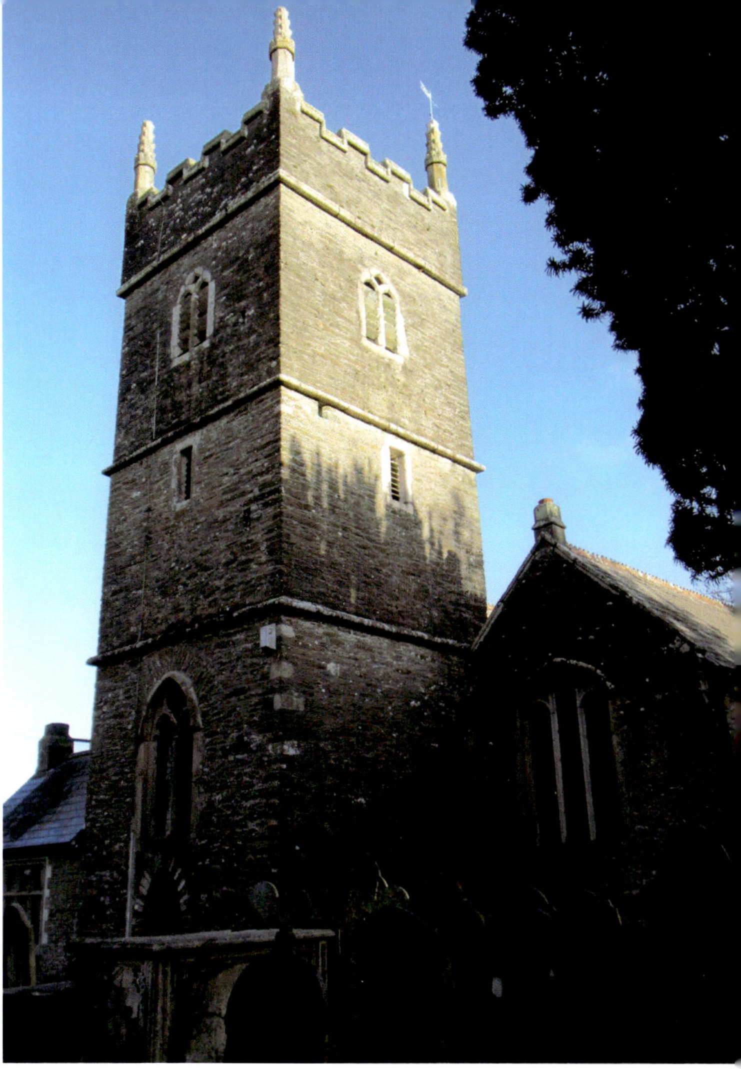

The tower of Higher St Budeaux Church.

building was just a small wattle church, but later a permanent stone church was built, just before the Norman invasion, and was dedicated to Budoc.

In the early Tudor period, there were demands for a bigger church to be built at St Budeaux. It was completed in 1563, five years into the reign of Queen Elizabeth I. In 1569, the church saw the marriage of Sir Francis Drake to Mary Newman.

During the Civil War, Plymouth and its surrounding villages such as St Budeaux had sworn an oath to fight and die for the Parliamentarian cause. However, in Cornwall, the people supported the Royalist cause and made raids across the water on parts of St Budeaux. For a time, the church at Higher St Budeaux was used as a garrison by the Royalists. On 16 April 1644, Lieutenant Colonel Martin sent 600 musketeers, with 120 horses, to attack the 500 Cavaliers stationed at St Budeaux. Because of a mistake made by guides, the horses went one way and the attacking party went another way. Nevertheless, the foot soldiers arrived at the church, saw off the enemy and captured the church tower.

On 27 December 1644, St Budeaux was again the scene of much bloodshed. From Kinterbury, the Roundheads marched towards the church, now a garrison for the Parliamentarians, and fought for an hour and a half before the church was recaptured. During the siege of Plymouth by the Royalists, the inhabitants of St Budeaux took provisions into town for the men and their horses. After the battle, the church was little more than a wreck and it wasn't restored until 1655.

Road widening in 1910 led to the discovery of cannonballs within the hedges near to the church.

Bibliography

Books

Tait, Derek, *A–Z of Plymouth* (Amberley Publishing, 2020)
Tait, Derek, *Devonport Through Time* (Amberley Publishing, 2013)
Derek, Tait, *Images of England: Plymouth* (The History Press, 2003)
Tait, Derek, *Plymouth at War* (The History Press, 2006)
Robinson, Chris, *Plymouth's Historic Barbican* (Pen & Ink, 2007)
Robinson, Chris, *Plymouth in the 70s* (Pen & Ink, 2015)
Tait, Derek, *St Budeaux* (Driftwood Coast Publishing, 2009)
Robinson, Chris, *Victorian Plymouth* (Pen & Ink, 2016)

Websites

Chris Robinson's Plymouth at www.chrisrobinson.co.uk
Devonport online at www.devonportonline.co.uk
Stephen Johnson's Cyberheritage site at https://www.facebook.com/hiddenheritageofficial/

Acknowledgements

Thanks to all the people who have helped me with research and have supplied photos and encouragement over the years including Stephen Johnson, Chris Robinson, Wesley Ashton, Marshall Ware and Eric Webb. Thanks also to Tina Cole and Tilly and Sadie who have accompanied me on my many journeys and photo shoots.

About the Author

Derek Tait has written over sixty books on subjects including social history, nostalgia, childhood, the First and Second World Wars, Houdini, Singapore and local history. He was born in Plymouth in 1961 and spent his early years in Singapore and Malaysia. He has written several books about his time there, including *Sampans, Banyans and Rambutans* and *Memories of Singapore and Malaya*. Other works include *1950s Childhood*, *1960s Childhood*, *A 1970s Childhood*, *The Great Houdini: His British Tours* and *Butlins: An Illustrated History*, as well as many books in the Through Time series for Amberley Publishing.